HALF A BANANA

HALF A BANANA

The diary of a Gurkha officer
imprisoned by the Japanese
Changi, 1942 – 1945

Peter Kemmis Betty

compiled by Richard Kemmis Betty

CHARLCOMBE BOOKS

Charlcombe Books
125 Garnet Street, Bristol BS3 3JH
Tel: 01174 523760

Published 2025

ISBN: 978 1 7399293 7 4

Printed and bound in Great Britain by
CPI Group, Chippenham, Wiltshire

This book is dedicated to
Peter Kemmis Betty and Alec Ogilvie

They both had so much respect for the Gurkhas
and their fun-loving approach to life.

Pokhara with Machapuchare and Annapurna as a back drop.
Painting by Gemma Kemmis Betty, 1965

Profits from this book

A significant proportion of any profits from the sale of 'Half a Banana' will be donated to Pahar Trust Nepal to support the education of Nepali and Gurkha children.

Pahar Trust Nepal is a UK-registered charity committed to supporting school projects in the foothills of the Himalayas. Its mission is to build safe, durable schools that create a positive and inspiring environment for students to learn.

Founded in 1991 by two former Queen's Gurkha Engineers, Pahar Trust Nepal has successfully built and renovated over 180 schools, benefiting countless lives along the way.

If you would like to find out more about Pahar Trust Nepal please visit:
www.pahar-trust.org

MY FATHER'S DIARY

Since the inception of this book, everyone involved has been so helpful – many thanks to all

For years my father had never spoken about being a prisoner of war. Then, one day, out of the blue, he presented my wife, Victoria, and me with various papers that he had tidied away some years before. Among them was the diary he had written during his time in Changi. There was no expectation for us to do anything with it right away; my father was simply aware that Victoria had recently acquired a new typewriter and had time on her hands: we had just moved to Herefordshire and rented a small cottage in the middle of the countryside to be nearer to my work.

A couple of years later my father asked Victoria if she might type up his diary. The handwriting was small and faint, making the task slow and laborious. At the time, I was hesitant to read it myself, as accounts of those years were so often harrowing and distressing. Since Victoria was transcribing rather than truly reading the diary, she was not absorbing much of it either, so we never discussed it.

With the finished document finally in hand, I can clearly remember arriving at my parents' house for Sunday lunch. Almost the first thing I asked my father was why he owned a Japanese car and a Japanese television. His response took me by surprise: "I have a great deal of respect for the Japanese." He was deeply grateful for the work Victoria had done, but the diary was not spoken of again and was quietly filed away in his desk.

Over time my younger brother, Charles, took responsibility for the family papers, having lived with our father in his later years. As the 75th Anniversary of VJ Day fell during Peter's 100th year, Charles arranged for Peter to be interviewed by the BBC for a Radio 4 programme that aired in August of that year. The diary was to see the light of day once more, less than a year before Peter's death.

Charles arranged for copies of the typed version to be given out at Peter's funeral, with one copy donated to the Gurkha Museum in Winchester. When Peter's house was sold and Charles moved to Germany, my youngest brother, David, and I took on responsibility for the family papers. Embarrassingly, the diary remained filed away, unread, for another eight years.

The idea to publish my father's Changi diary came to me in May 2024, while listening to the many remarkable stories shared during the

D-Day 80th Anniversary celebrations. As I was clearing out our cluttered study, I came across the original diary. Almost instantly, I knew the right thing to do was to try to publish it – it couldn't stay hidden away in a drawer for ever. A chain of events unfolded that quickly led me down a path I couldn't easily turn away from.

After discussing the idea with my family and receiving a surprising amount of encouragement, I mentioned it to Anthony Gibson. Anthony had written books on a wide range of subjects, and he kindly suggested I meet his publisher, Stephen Chalke. Anthony, Stephen and I first met in late August. During the meeting I explained the story, and despite his busy schedule Stephen generously agreed to make time to publish it.

My brother, David, suggested I get advice from Tom Bradby, the journalist who currently presents ITN's *News at Ten*. The Bradbys were family friends, and Tom had known my father for many years. Despite his incredibly busy schedule – dealing with Middle East issues, American elections, government budgets and more – Tom met me for breakfast. His advice inspired me to take a more committed approach to the project, though it never felt like a burden.

Almost everyone I spoke to about the diary had the same initial reaction: 'Oh gosh, how terrible.' This led me to explain that it was a very different story from most accounts of prisoners-of-war held by the Japanese. The diary is not a grim read; far from it – it is a testament to survival and the resilience of the human spirit. The reaction was one of considerable interest, with many people offering advice and, from this, the right contacts began to emerge. Given that my father was a Gurkha officer, it felt natural to start with the Gurkha contacts I knew.

A close friend, William Shuttlewood, who is Chairman of the 2nd Goorkhas, put me in touch with the team at the Gurkha Museum. Initially this was for research purposes, but this quickly grew into a more substantial collaboration, especially with their plans to mark the 80th Anniversary of VJ Day in the latter half of 2025. Everyone at the Gurkha Museum has been incredibly supportive.

It was a steep learning curve, gathering information and, most importantly, gaining a deeper understanding of the diary. From the diary and a number of old family letters, I soon realised there was more to the story. To explore this further, I made contact with Adam Ogilvie, the eldest son of Peter's great friend and fellow prisoner, Alec.

When we first met, Adam brought along some fascinating

memorabilia of his father's time in Changi. Our discussions confirmed to me a hidden sub-plot. Adam's input has been a tremendous help.

With this deeper understanding of the story, a family holiday to Singapore and Malaya was planned for November 2024. A chance conversation at a drinks party resulted in being given a number of most helpful contacts, and we ended up meeting Liz Coward at the Changi Museum. Liz, one of the senior guides, gave us a deeply moving and fascinating tour; we spent five hours at the museum, visited the chapel and walked much of the area, finishing up at Changi Village. The area is vastly different to eighty years ago, now bordered by the vast expanse of Changi International Airport. The thirty acres of gardens have been replaced by runways.

The prison gaol has been expanded and modernised, though parts of the old walls exist. Some of the old buildings are no longer in use, but the topography remains largely unchanged, still dominated by Temple Hill, with views down to the sea through large tropical trees. Most of the jungle stretches down to the water's edge.

Safely back in the UK, the research moved into top gear. Particular thanks go to John Harrop and Nick Hinton. They were just completing a publication on the history of the 2nd King Edward's Own Goorkha Rifles and therefore I was able to cross reference their material with other archive records on the Malaysian campaign. A very helpful visit to the National Army Museum provided further insight, clarifying the different accounts of the fighting that led up to the surrender of Singapore.

The structure of the book was coming together, and it was time to consider a suitable cover. It wasn't until visiting a friend's house that I noticed a painting that matched the style I had in mind. This led to a meeting with the local artist, Nick Andrew of Bull Mill Studio, Crockerton. Nick immediately understood what was needed and, most importantly, was fascinated by this very different story. The result is the excellent book cover, which captures its three main elements: gardens, Gurkhas and the subtle hint of the Japanese flag.

A big thank you goes to my family: to my wife, Victoria, for putting up with the endless hours I spent camped at my lap top; to my eldest son, Jonathan, for his wonderful work improving the flow of the story and correcting my amateurish English; and to my youngest son, Alexander, for using his marketing expertise to raise the book's profile before and after its launch.

Richard Kemmis Betty, Dorset, April 2025

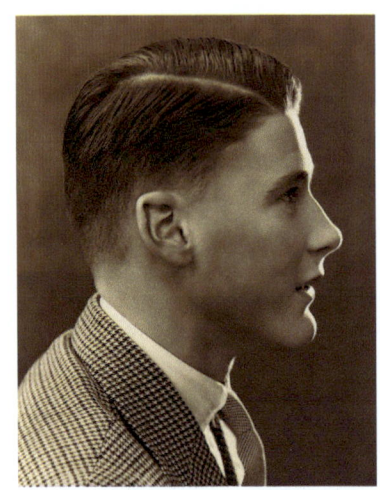

Peter Kemmis Betty

Alec Ogilvie

THE START OF A DEEP FRIENDSHIP

That Peter Kemmis Betty and Alec Ogilvie knew each other as teenagers is not, in itself, particularly remarkable. That they would later serve in the same regiment during the Second World War and subsequently spend considerable time together as prisoners in Changi would have been unimaginable to them as children.

Peter's father, Hubert, had been a well decorated army officer, serving as a Lieutenant Colonel with the Royal Canadian Regiment during the First World War. Unfortunately, he was gassed early in the conflict and invalided back to London where he then worked in the Canadian Record Office.

Not long after Hubert's return, in 1916, Peter Kemmis Betty was born, the youngest of three siblings. Within six years the family had moved to Switzerland, partly due to Hubert's ill health and partly because they felt their prospects were limited in England at the time. During their time in Switzerland, Peter, alongside his older brother Mervyn (born in 1908), became a skilled skier, sparking his enduring love for the mountains. He reluctantly hung up his skis for the final time at the age of 85.

Upon the family's return to England after seven years, they set up home in Camberley, not far from the Ogilvie family, whom they had yet to meet. The Ogilvies, having recently returned from India, had taken an apartment at Frimley Hall. With both families new to the area and sharing similar sporting interests, it was perhaps only a matter of time before their paths crossed. The Pantiles was the venue, a popular local tea room with tennis courts and a swimming pool, where the families spent much of their time and quickly formed a close friendship.

Like Peter Kemmis Betty, Alec Ogilvie spent a considerable portion of his early childhood abroad. He was born in Oxfordshire in 1917 but then spent much of his early childhood in India, growing up in Bengal before moving back to England for his education. Whilst Peter and Alec attended separate colleges, Bradfield and Cheltenham respectively, their shared experience of boarding school in the 1920s would have inevitably subjected them both to what could be a harsh, demanding environment. In their first few years the boys would have effectively acted as personal servants, or 'fags', to the senior students, performing chores or running errands. Stepping out of line would most often be met with punishments, both from their seniors and from teachers, some of the latter being particularly feared for their liberal use of the cane.

As demanding as the surroundings could be at times, the conditions trained children how to adapt to adversity, to deal with abuse and, perhaps most importantly, how to avoid potential confrontation in the first place by conforming to a system. For many the circumstances were unpleasant, but it is not a stretch to see how useful such an education might prove to be for Peter, Alex and others in their later lives. It instilled in them a respect for both seniors and juniors alike, a keen awareness of the standards they were expected to meet and an understanding of the boundaries within which they had to operate. Beyond discipline and resilience, school was also where Alec developed his love for acting and Peter his passion for choral music – interests that would remain with them for years to come.

When Alec and Peter left school, in 1932 and 1936 respectively, they were well prepared to face the challenges of the wider world, though only a special foresight could have wholly prepared them for the global conflict ahead. Initially Alec spent a few years working as an accountant in London, before returning to India within three years. He joined the Andrew Yule company in Calcutta in 1935, becoming the seventh generation of his family to work or serve in India. Peter was equally influenced by his family, particularly his father, choosing to join the military shortly after school. His brother, Mervyn, was already serving as a Royal Artillery officer on the North-West Frontier. Their sister, Barbara, had married a Gurkha officer in the Indian Army.

Thankfully for their mother, Peter began his military career very close to home at the Royal Military Academy Sandhurst (RMAS). He spoke fondly of his time there, hugely enjoying the numerous sports on offer, at which he regularly excelled. All officers were taught to ride, and he was always pleasantly surprised to be chosen for the 'top ride'. A number of the winters were so cold that he was able to arrange games of ice hockey on RMAS's Lower Lake, a pastime that his Canadian father happily encouraged. Peter was, though, especially proud of his gymnastic skills.

Whilst still at Sandhurst, Peter was required to chose a regiment. In a BBC interview, at the age of 99, he explained that various factors led him towards the Gurkhas. However, he acknowledged that there was an element of chance, as officers had to be 'accepted' since they were hand-picked. With his brother already serving in the Indian Army as an Artillery Officer and his sister married to a 5th Gurkha, being accepted into the 2nd Gurkhas was ideal. Furthermore, he believed that life in the Indian Army offered more opportunities and, crucially, that it was easier to live on officer's pay in India.

Peter was commissioned as an officer in the army in January 1936. Before joining the 2nd Gurkhas he had to learn the ropes, as he put it, and briefly joined the 1st Battalion of the Royal Fusiliers (City of London Regiment) in Delhi for just over a year. He spent his time gleaning what he could about military life in India and, importantly, learning Urdu and Hindustani from a most wonderful 'munshi' (teacher).

In March 1937 Peter was appointed to the 2nd Gurkhas. After a brief period in Chittagong, the battalion returned to its home in Dehra Dun, an attractive Himalayan hill town not far from Nathan in Sirmoor State, where the regiment originated and which lent the battalion its alternative name, 'The Sirmoor Rifles'. Peter recalled that "these time in the foothills of the Himalayas were wonderful" – although the task of 'opening' roads at 7,000 ft with snow on the ground, still dressed in the Gurkha's heavily starched shorts, does appear less appealing. Furthermore, "you had to keep your wits about you as there was always a risk of being shot up." The battalion was gradually acclimatising to 'mountain warfare'.

In the same BBC interview he was asked of his opinion of the Gurkhas in those early days. His response was telling: "I immediately realised I was in the company of special people." He soon developed a great attachment to those with him and was drawn to the Gurkhas' fundamental desire to enjoy life: "During Dussehra celebrations they would put on stage shows. They were called 'Joka' parties, taking off the British Officers, and very good at it they were."

Unfortunately the fun times were cut short by the start of the Second World War in September 1939. Just over a month later, aged just 23, he accompanied the 2nd King Edward VII's Own Gurkha Rifles Battalion to Bannu, on the North-West Frontier, as part of 4th Infantry Brigade. The battalion subsequently moved to Razmak as part of Waziristan Garrison where Peter was appointed Adjutant.

Alec Ogilvie had been working in Calcutta up to this point, but upon hearing the call for volunteers to join the army, stepped forward. Following his Officer Training at Secunderabad he applied and was 'accepted' to join 2nd Gurkha Rifles (2GR). Peter and Alec were to meet again because, as a newly commissioned officer, Alec joined the same battalion in May 1941. Alec Ogilvie was well regarded and was given the rank of Captain despite his relative lack of military experience. He took over from Peter as Adjutant.

Although much of the British military's focus was on the German threat, the Japanese soon emerged as a significant factor. As far back as 1934 Japanese agents had been active in the bazaars of China, Indonesia, and Malaya trying to gain support to drive 'white races' back to Suez. When France fell and Great Britain stood alone in Europe, Japan saw its opportunity to act. The cost of sustaining their war machine had weakened the Japanese economy, and they now set their sights on the riches of South-East Asia. Their primary targets were the rubber plantations and tin mines of Malaya and, most importantly, the oil fields of Sarawak.

In July 1941 orders were received to mobilise. Due to the increasing German threat and their rapid expansion, the expectation was that the 2nd Gurkhas would be sent to fight in the Western Desert of Africa. Certainly, all the training the battalion had been given was for 'open' warfare in desert conditions. The battalion moved to Bombay where they embarked on the SS Egra. Sixteen British officers (Woollcombe, Evans, Kemmis Betty, Ogilvie, Dallas-Smith, Hancock, Magee, Bucknole, Lucas, Henderson, Cooper, Elton, Coombe, Jenkins, Lovett, Skene – and Subedar-Major Hari Singh Bohra), 22 Gurkha officers and 831 Gurkhas set sail.

The battalion's ultimate destination quickly became a subject of debate since some officers spotted that their issued camouflage scrim netting was jungle green, not desert brown. Not long after leaving Bombay, the special sealed orders were opened, revealing that the battalion was destined not for the Middle East but for Port Swettenham (now Port Klang) in Malaya, around 40km south-west of Kuala Lumpur. Peter's attitude to the change of plan "was one of quite a lot of interest". He welcomed the idea of seeing a different part of the world.

The battalion disembarked on 3rd September 1941. With their vehicles delayed on another ship, the journey up to Ipoh was by train. The last few miles from the impressive Ipoh Station to their camp were completed in Australian military lorries. Their new base was to be at the Canning Estate, a rubber estate two miles to the north of Ipoh. This is where the ordered lines of rubber trees meet jungle, a very different world. The Gurkhas' home was in the mountains of the Himalayas. Instead of the dry heat of India and the cold nights of the mountains, they were hit with the tropical warmth and humidity of Malaya. The temperature in the day was always hovering around 30C and even at night never dropped below 24C. They had to rethink and prepare for conditions that they had not encountered before.

On the train journey they would have seen a very green world, initially of rubber plantations – tree upon tree of meticulously ordered and well run estates. The first part of the journey was quite flat, with a number of large muddy rivers meandering past the window. As they moved north from Kuala Lumpur the mood of the countryside began to change. Although predominantly following one of the major rivers, the landscape became increasingly hilly and the neatly formed plantations gave way to dense, impregnable jungle. Nearing Ipoh, they would have quickly noticed some other-worldly formations: limestone outcrops that seemed to rear up precipitously from the dark green jungle.

The train journey took them north from Kuala Lumpur, past Slim River and then Kampar. Within months of their arrival in Malaya, and far sooner than they might have predicted, they would see many of these vistas again as they pushed south, attempting to stall the rapid advance of the Japanese invasion forces.

When they set up camp in Ipoh they were part of 28th Indian Brigade (the reserve to 2nd Corps), in effect a Gurkha Brigade since it combined with the Indian Army Regiments who also recruited Gurkha soldiers. The battalion settled into a two-month period of intensive training through October and November 1941. The spirit of the Gurkhas was strong so they were able to make the most of a tense environment. Fortuitously their location was close to ideal. Ipoh's position at the centre of Malaya's tin and rubber industries meant that it was a vibrant town with, amongst other amenities, decent bars and a private members' club overlooking a polo ground. There was even a race course, with race meetings that took place at least twice a month.

Alec wrote of those first days in Ipoh. The first thing that struck everyone was the amazing cleanliness of the town. The men said the surrounding hills reminded them of Nepal. The camp consisted of a series of wooden huts scattered amongst the rubber trees. The accommodation was good; however, living in a rubber estate produces a peculiar state of mind and body which is brought about by the almost complete absence of sunlight. The trees were sacred and not to be cut under any circumstances.

On 6th December, following the recce of a defensive position at Jitra, 250km north of Ipoh, the officers had somehow persuaded the Commanding Officer (CO) that it would be acceptable to go to a race meeting. The CO instructed them that they must telephone into the guard room every half hour so, following each race, they checked in for any updates. When they phoned in after the fifth race they were given orders to return urgently to barracks. Intelligence suggested that the Japanese had begun their advance south.

Then on 7th December the Japanese attacked Pearl Harbour, and the following day landings were reported just north of the border in Siam and at Kota Bahru in Malaya. Peter left with a small advance party to prepare the positions in Jitra.

On the 9th and 10th December Peter led the battalion into their company positions. Jitra was only 30 kms from the Siam border where the Japanese were expected to cross into Malaya. The landscape was a mixture of rubber estates and jungle: the former well ordered, with some big clearings, so it was easy to move through, the latter far too dense to make meaningful headway.

Peter reported in his interview with the BBC: "We were in position for only 24 hours before the Japanese attacked our positions. They came down the road on bikes and with light tanks. They came in at night 'shrieking', shouting and letting off fire crackers. It was not easy to know how to deal with them. We didn't want to expend all our ammunition firing aimlessly at the noises in the dark so we waited until the targets could be clearly identified. We held our position for three days and then the order came to withdraw under darkness."

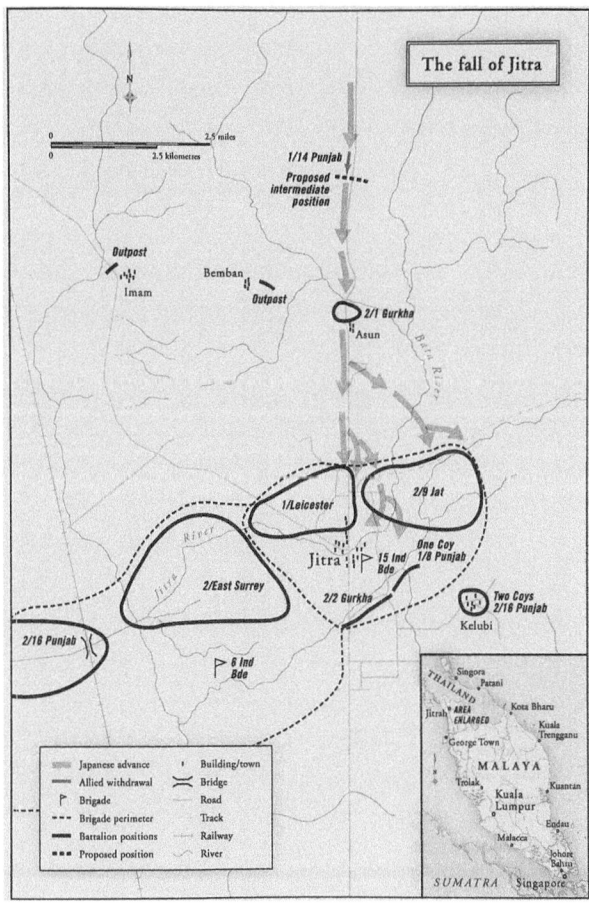

An extract from the citation for Havildar (Gurkha rank equivalent to Sergeant) Diwat Pun described some extraordinary courage. At Jitra on 12th December the enemy supported by tanks and heavy mortar fire had broken through and overrun the forward battalions. They then heavily engaged the 2/2nd Gurkhas who had a few hours previously been ordered to occupy a semi-prepared area in reserve. Havildar commanded one of the forward platoons. His platoon was first subjected to intense mortar and then fiercely attacked. Many of his men were young soldiers, in battle for the first time, and were shaken by the disaster they had seen to the unit in front of them, stragglers of which were passing through their position. Havildar, with complete disregard for his own safety, constantly moved about his front, under heavy mortar and small arms fire, encouraging his section posts. He repaired stoppages in Bren guns and fired each in turn himself to restore confidence, and generally encouraged his men by his own magnificent example. It was entirely due to him that his platoon was able to repel all attacks and maintain its position until ordered to withdraw.

"We did not feel good about withdrawing"

Extracting a battalion from a defensive position when under attack was a difficult task. 2GR was tasked to cover the withdrawal of the 15th and 28th Brigades who had been ordered to fall back behind the Kedah River which was 12 miles to the south. After three days of fighting the next problem was the lack of transport. 2GR successfully extracted themselves and moved to south of the river Langgar when the bridge was successfully blown. Now exhausted they had to march another 18 miles south to Jehun.

Almost as soon as they arrived they were ordered to fall back to take up positions on the 14th/15th December at Gurun, which was a further six miles south. Bob Skene engaged with the enemy at Gurun before falling back, the bridge being blown once they had passed.

Following abandonment of their blocking positions at Gurun they arrived at Sungai Patani on the evening 15th December. With little to no sleep or food, permission was granted to withdraw a further 14 miles to south of the Muda river. Of 28th Brigade only 2GR was intact. 1st/2nd Gurkhas had been cut off three times and were reduced to just 300 men.

On 16th December they travelled by train to a small village on the edge of a rubber estate at Parit Buntar. Peter mentioned how appreciative everyone was when the village provided tea and biscuits. The village was mostly Chinese and they did this at a considerable risk.

British troops being fed by Chinese villagers, by Leo Rawlings

Further orders came to withdraw to the Perak River, which meant another march south to Bagan Serai. Once there, they were joined by an additional 90 men and received mortars and light machine guns to replace those lost in battle. On taking up positions a new order came in that put the Gurkhas on the road again. The next withdrawal was 60 miles south-east to Sungei Siput to the east of the Perak River where they took up a position as divisional reserve. The advance of the Japanese forces that landed at Singora and Patani had taken them south converging just east of Taiping and not far from Ipoh. This forced a further withdrawal of 2GR back through Ipoh and then a further 40 miles to Chenderaing, where a line of defence was being prepared in the Kampar region.

This was a hilly region with dense jungle and any attack would be forced to route through Chenderaing. The defensive position was excellent.

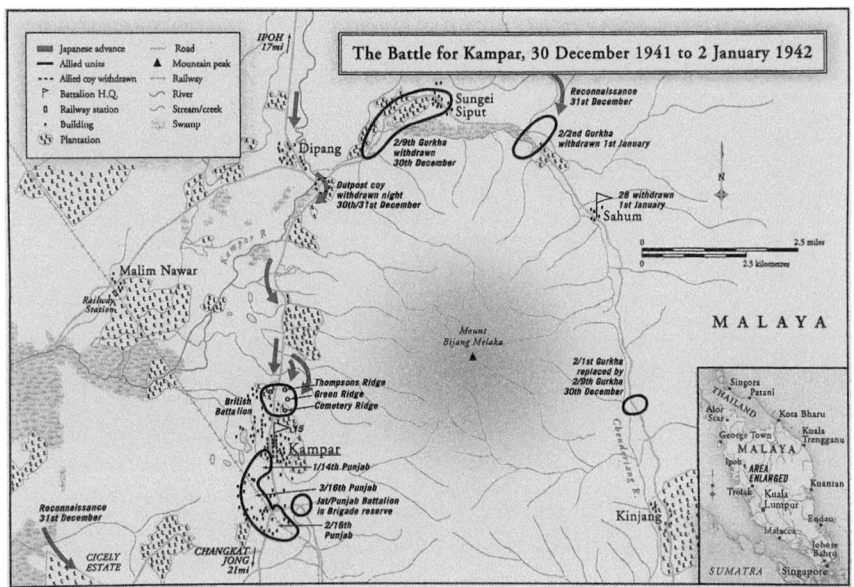

The Battle for Kampar, 30 December 1941 to 2 January 1942

My father's notes suggested that at Kampar the 2nd Gurkhas had their greatest success in inflicting a great number of Japanese casualties but, ultimately, that they were frustrated once more by being asked to withdraw.

In Havildar Dewat Pun's citation from Chenderaing, it stated that he was holding the extreme right of the main position. His section's own right flank was bordered by thick jungle through which the enemy was attempting to infiltrate in an effort to outflank the whole position. Whilst on a fighting patrol his platoon encountered a Japanese reconnaissance patrol. Attacking immediately, Havildar Dewat Pun killed a number of the enemy and they put the remainder to flight. He returned with invaluable identifications and a marked map taken off a Japanese Officer he had killed. His initiative and courage was of the highest order, setting a magnificent example to all who saw him.

The 2nd Gurkhas were positioned east of Sungei Siput when orders were received to cover the withdrawal of the remainder of 28th Indian Brigade. Peter was in command of a detachment holding a vitally important bridge over the Sungai Dipang River. His position came under heavy enemy fire but the bridge had to be held until it could be blown. They were successful in preventing the Japanese from over-running the position and taking the bridge. For his bravery and for the courage of his Gurkha detachment, Peter was awarded the Military Cross (MC).

Peter Kemmis Betty's Military Cross

From the citation:

On 29th Dec. 41 he was commanding the detachment holding the bridge over the Sungai Dipang. The bridge-head area was under heavy artillery, mortar and later small arms fire. When all troops had passed in accordance with orders, he skilfully extricated his force. Three times the demolition charge failed to destroy the bridge – three times he led his detachment forward again to cover the Sapper demolition party, which was eventually successful.

It was some years later that my father spoke of the defence of the bridge, and, with a great deal of humour, he mentioned that it wasn't the enemy fire that concerned them most but the shrieking noise the Japanese soldiers made when attacking.

Inevitably, instructions came for another withdrawal, back to Slim River.

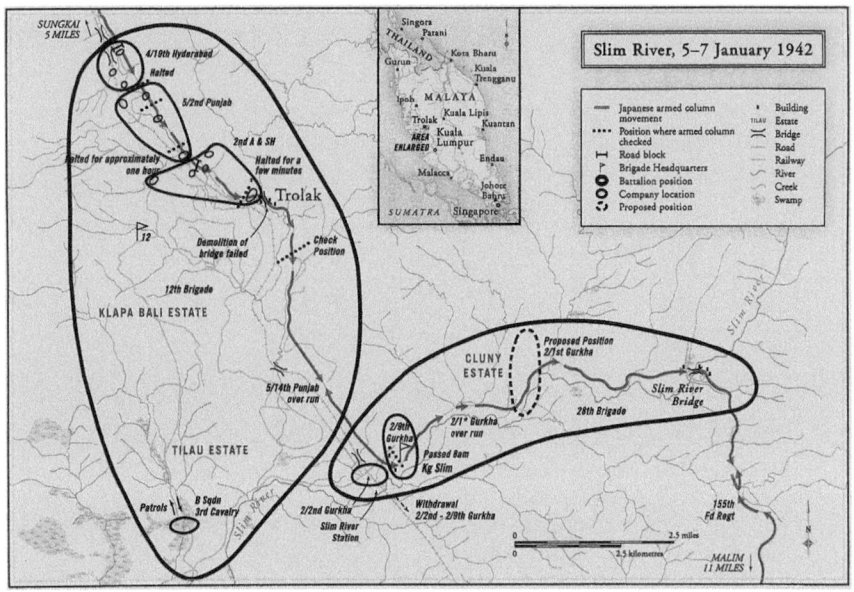

At Slim River, despite fierce resistance, the battalion was outflanked. To compound its struggles, the bridge was blown, leaving the men stranded on the wrong side and forcing them to make their own way across the river. Many soldiers were drowned and much equipment was lost. Peter made some brief notes about Slim River that succinctly sum up the disaster: 'The bridge was blown too soon, leaving many troops on the other side – many men were drowned. Two Companies 'lost' – split up into small parties. They walked for 15 miles down the river line heading south during the night. Men were completely exhausted. Of the 2 companies lost: 3 Battalion Officers, 6 Gurkha Officers, and 196 Gurkha soldiers.'

Amid the adversity, two extraordinary acts of bravery emerged. Unlike many soldiers Pirag, the masalchi (cook), was a competent swimmer. Time and time again he waded back into the river to help those soldiers who couldn't make it across on their own. Subedar Kalu Chhetri, undaunted by enemy mortar and tank fire, coolly organised a section to form a bridgehead, allowing so many to be extricated. For this and his leadership throughout the campaign he was awarded the Military Cross.

On 9th January the battalion was down to two Companies. They dug in, covering the bridge over Sungui Selangor and holding the position to allow other allied forces to cross. When the bridge was blown they climbed onto Australian lorries and moved down to Serendah 15 miles to the south. A month of intense fighting had passed, and 2GR were now half way down Malaya.

After a series of withdrawals, marked by courageous fighting to defend yet another bridge – this time over the Sungai Chook – the battalion was transported 100 miles south, eventually reaching Johore, the southernmost state of Malaya. They regrouped at Tampin, located just north of Malacca, and then embarked on another journey 125 miles south-east to their final position at Pontian Kechil, a mere 25 miles from the causeway into Singapore.

Letter to brother Mervyn, 21st January 1942

The letter was sent to Mervyn's last known address whilst on 'Active Service' and posted in the Perak region where they were fighting the Japanese. The envelope bears a 25c Malay stamp and is addressed to Maj M.F. Kemmis Betty at 26th Mountain Battery RA, Razmak, Waziristan, India. The letter was 'opened by censor' and redirected to Mervyn at the School of Artillery, Deolah. It is telling that Peter felt it important to get such a detailed letter off to his brother.

Very many apologies for not having communicated before now, but it has been a fast moving life with extremely little time for anything other than the caps! ...

Our Bde got a hell of a hammering right from the very start and we were only taken out of the immediate front line about a week ago (though where we are now threatens to become a front line any moment). It has been rather a tough business with no air or tanks ... The Japs were in the air almost the entire day dive bombing and machine gunning everything they saw ... The men took a long time to get over an episode about a month ago when half a dozen bombs fell slap in the middle of Bn HQ and *[cut out by censor]* a v. nasty mess.

We lost literally all our possessions except what we stood up in on one occasion when the gap tanks broke through and cut us off from our line of retreat. We were the wrong side of a river and had to abandon all our transport and get back across in single file over a blown up railway bridge – many of the men were drowned trying to cross lower down, that was followed by an all night march down the railway line not knowing where the hell the Japs were.

We had a couple of very 'warm' parties forming bridge heads with my Company and on the second occasion we were attacked in the half light, we had to blow the bridge in the middle of the battle and had difficulty getting the men back over the river – after which we were subjected to a most unpleasant dive bombing attack by about 4 planes lasting 40 mins or so – we were in a village with practically no cover & the Jap mortars coming over us at the same time. Anyway we got out of it O.K. with remarkably few casualties. I got hit by a bit of something in the back of the ear – bled profusely but turned out to be infinitesimally small.

The narrowest shave I had was on the 2nd or 3rd day of the show, right up north when I was fired upon by our own troops (an Indian Battalion) when returning to my Company position at night. Luckily I knew their Coy. Cmdr quite well and by shouting out bloody loud he heard me and stopped their fire ...

I rather envy you in Razmak! Did you get any skiing? P

So rapid was the Japanese advance that the local population remained completely unaware of the situation. Shops and bars were still open, and expatriates were still partying into the night. However, the urgency of the situation quickly became clear when stragglers from the fighting in the north began to appear, prompting a rush to close up shops and evacuate to Singapore.

The Japanese had broken through 40 miles to the north and the battalion came under heavy fire and attacks from enemy aircraft, luckily without any success. The battalion regrouped to cross the bridges at Pontian Besar and Pontian Kechil before they were blown. They had to withdraw nine miles to the east along the Skudal Road, skirting the swampy tip of the Johore peninsula.

At dawn on 31st January 1942, the order came to withdraw across the causeway into Singapore before it was also destroyed – a most dramatic event. Following this final withdrawal, the battalion was given the task of defending the large naval base on the north-east of the island, just 300 yards east of the causeway.

On 2nd February a Japanese aircraft crashed into one of the big oil tanks at the naval base and this became a marker for other Japanese bombers. On 5th February Japanese shelling had a direct hit on one of the large magazines and 10 Gurkhas were killed.

In his notes, Peter said that the Japanese crossed the straits to the left of the 2/2GR position on 6th and 7th February. The Australians were on the left flank and fell back, creating a big gap in defences. However, it wasn't until 9th February that they learned that the Australians had decided to retreat four miles inland, leaving 2GR exposed.

To add to the difficulties, 2GR's Commanding Officer, Lt.Col. Geoffrey Woollcombe, was suffering badly from infected tropical wounds, and so handed over command to Maj. Derek Robertson. 2GR took up an excellent position near Nee Soon village. This position at Bukit Timah was strategically strong, being on the highest hill on Singapore Island, some 500 feet up. Peter's opinion at the time was that they had more than an equal chance of holding this high ground.

15th February 1942 started with heavy artillery fire and air attack and then in the early afternoon a dispatch rider arrived with a message which said: '*At 1600 hours all troops under command will cease fire but will remain in their positions. If attacked by the enemy after 1600 hours the officer or non-commissioned officer in command of the party concerned will raise the white flag. There will be no destruction of arms or equipment but all secret papers and ciphers will be destroyed. Water and rations must be conserved. All money will be burned.'*

It was much to the annoyance of the men that the order to cease fire was given at all. In the BBC interview, Peter describes how "a sudden silence came over the land – you could have heard the birds singing. We just lay down and slept."

On 16th February, the battalion joined up with the other Gurkha units under command of the 28th Indian Brigade so that the Gurkhas could stay together in captivity. Peter explained that "we were separated from our Gurkha soldiers who were imprisoned in the South West of the Island. The officers were then marched 17 miles to Changi."

In the 2015 BBC interview, Peter was asked for his opinion of General Percival. As someone who disliked criticising others, his thoughts are telling: "He was a successful staff officer but not a commanding personality, no comparison with General Bill Slim."

Peter also explained that a major factor in the decision to surrender was the severe damage to Singapores's water supply. He expressed sympathy for General Percival, acknowledging the immense pressure he must have faced in making such a difficult choice.

*This map was published in the Japanese press in Tokyo on the day that their forces crossed
into Singapore. It not only highlights their level of preparedness but also reveals the extent
of their intelligence, as all the Allied key strategic positions were accurately marked.*

The Japanese planned well and their intelligence was good. They were
single-minded, and the objective of securing the oil fields of Sarawak,
Java and Indonesia was paramount. In their drive south they had left
small pockets of soldiers throughout Malaya. What they didn't plan for
was the sheer number of prisoners they would have to manage when
they reached Singapore. After the Allied surrender many of the Japanese
frontline soldiers soon moved on to tackle their next objective: the oil
fields on the islands of Java and Sarawak. It meant there were few to
manage the prisoners.

Changi prisoner-of-war camp was located on the eastern tip of
Singapore Island, covering a huge area of 22 square kilometres. It
included the relatively small Changi gaol where mostly civilians were
imprisoned. Over the course of the conflict, more than 100,000 prisoners
of war passed through Changi, many on their way up to the Thai-Burma
railway, where conditions were far worse than at Changi. Alec and Peter
could count themselves among the lucky few to spend their entire time

at Changi, avoiding the gruelling labour camps and extreme conditions of the railway, which claimed the lives of so many who were sent there.

During the first two months of captivity, Sook Ching (meaning purging through cleansing) took place under the noses of the prisoners. The Japanese massacred thousands of Chinese, with these atrocities occurring on the small island behind Changi. There were also random acts of brutality, often against innocent civilians.

*

The diary was written by Peter Kemmis Betty during his three and a half years of captivity under the Japanese. It offers a detailed account of what it was like to be a British prisoner of war in Changi.

Not everything could be recorded in his diary. Many prisoners took considerable risks. The trade 'under the wire' with the local Chinese to purchase 'smokes' or food seemed to go unnoticed. Writing a diary would not have been looked upon kindly, especially if it had included criticism of the guards. Some prisoners were known to have taken even greater risks. If found with a camera or a radio, the punishment would have been harsh.

The first weeks of captivity were particularly stressful, with many prisoners enduring harsh treatment. In order for the few guards to keep control, discipline was dealt out in a harsh manner. It took a couple of months for the running of the camp to settle down, and during this period anyone stepping out of line or disrespecting the Japanese command was punished. For this reason, Peter's first notes were not made until 26th July. My father, when asked about this period before he put pen to paper, would just say: "You knew where you stood."

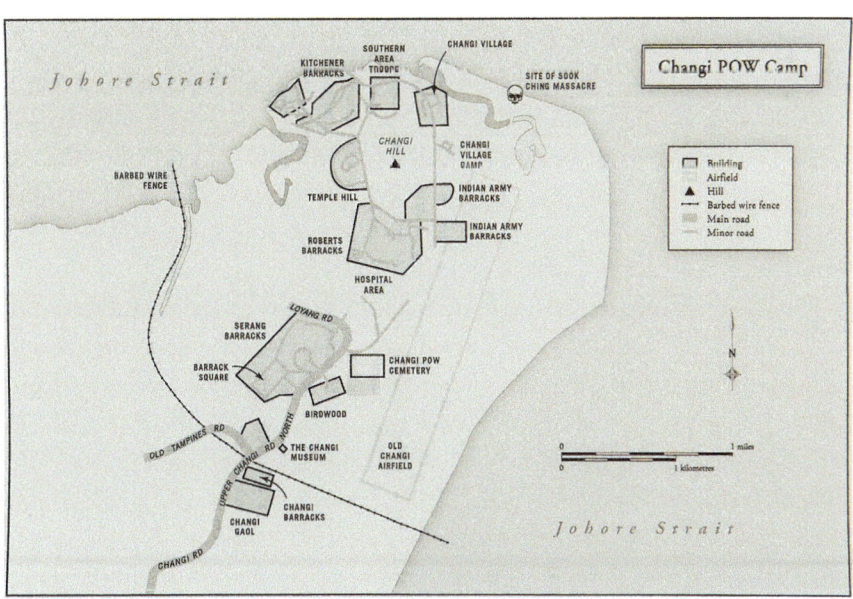

Simplified diagram of Changi where over 17,000 Allied prisoners were held 1942-45 – N.E. side of Singapore Island.

DIARY OF A PRISONER OF WAR

Boxed sections are background information, not part of the diary

Sunday 26 July 1942

Having been nearly six months in captivity it has occurred to me that
it would be useful to get something down on paper about our life and
conditions here in this camp. Not that the life is packed with incident
very far from it – but it is sure to be of some interest to those at home and
in India who are bound to ply us with countless questions. Perhaps this
may obviate saying it all many times over and also make letter writing an
easier matter. I shall not attempt to write this strictly according to the
order of events but from now on I hope to produce a weekly letter.

I shall begin, then, by giving you a picture of our building and
surroundings. The Camp is situated in the east corner of Singapore
Island and is composed of five separate areas.

Ours is probably the best situated, about 400 of us being quartered in
the R.A. Officers Mess, a massive imposing building perched on the top
of a small hill about 100 feet above the surrounding countryside, from
where we get an immediate view over the Singapore Straits, to the north,
and the open sea to the east and south. I often feel we are very lucky to
have this view of water and distant hills, whereas others down below may
perpetually be looking out on some war-blasted building or drab parade
ground. There are nine of us occupying a medium sized room designed
normally for one officer; this may sound very tight but it is not at all too
bad and anyway, we have got used to it.

We have a little bit of verandah which is to all intents and purposes our private sitting-room, used throughout the day for reading, card games, etc. – and fortunately we all get on extraordinarily well with each other. None of us had any possessions on arrival, bar a few items of necessary clothing, so bed-making became the chief occupation in the early days – and some very remarkable beds there are, made from every conceivable piece of junk. Some of the more idle are confirmed floor-sleepers, one of whom in our room uses the Saville Row-made coats belonging to the peace-time occupants of the room as his mattress (Alec Ogilvie!).

Even now the first few weeks seem rather hazy. We had little or no money and the cigarettes which we had brought in with us very soon ran out. For three or four days we fed like lords until we were put onto the basic ration of rice, when we had to start spinning out as long as we could all the tinned goods which we had been able to bring into the camp.

From then on, as it is now, FOOD was the main consideration.

People soon discovered it was possible to get hold of tinned foods and cigarettes from the Chinese and Malays and these they then resold within the camp – and so the 'Black Market', as it was called, became a going concern.

The average price for ten English cigarettes was $1.50 and a tin of bully beef costs anything up to $5. We fortunately managed to get small loans of money from the wealthy, and well do I remember the tense excitement with which four of us sat down one evening to our first Black Market meal consisting of one roll of bread (divided into four), a small tin of margarine and a tin of salmon, working out at exactly $2 per head (the roll cost a dollar).

A great asset to life were the Chinese cigarettes which were gradually filtered into the camp in increasing quantities. They cost only 30 cents for 20 and at the time I am writing we smoke nothing else – in fact I now prefer them to the cheap English Virginians of which we get a free ration of 10 per week.

We have had a proper Mess Committee running for a long time now. The Kitchen is staffed entirely by Officers who steadily become more apt at disguising rice in more palatable forms. We supplement the small jap flour ration by grinding the raw rice down into rice flour, thus being able to produce bread and pastry in greater quantity (the two types of flour being mixed together). This rice grinding was a very laborious process in the early days, bottles being used on marble slabs but our R.E. brethren soon got busy and now we are fully mechanised – just feed with rice, turn the handle and out comes the flour. Incidentally the main component of our recently made bread oven is a large abandoned electrical transformer!

About six weeks ago the Japanese started giving us a small Amenity Grant of $7.50 per head per month. Out of this 75c goes to the Hospital and $2 to the Mess. A properly organised Canteen Service is also functioning whereby we can get, at almost rock-bottom peace-time prices, all the more common types of tinned foods, English sauces, jam, marmalade, dripping, marmite, etc., and Chinese cigarettes at 10c for 10. So life would be grand – as far as the stomach is concerned – if we had a few hundred dollars to play with, but it's not quite so easy with only 4.75 dollars a months. I seem to have been talking far too much about food but we find it such an absorbing subject here!

We were surprised to be allowed almost unrestricted movement inside the main camp area for about the first three weeks, before we had to put up our own barbed wire perimeter. During that time we used to go down swimming in the bathing 'pagar' at any time we wished – quite a large social gathering – and a very pleasant spot. I even had a couple of evenings' tennis.

But all that ceased when our wire went up.

Nowadays all movement outside camp areas is done in formed bodies and each party has to have a special Japanese flag with it, for use as a pass. We are allowed to go sea-bathing every Monday morning but it is seldom worth going down unless the tide happens to be right up.

With regard to entertainment, we are possibly not as well off, musically, as other areas, there being no piano up here to form the basis of a band or concert party.

But in 'Southern Area', just over the road, there is an exceptionally good group of variety performers who have up to date put on three really first class shows, each having had a run of about a month and showing three or four evenings in the week. There are two or three professionals amongst them and an orchestra of about ten strong. Some of their acts would be worthy of the London Hippodrome.

Then there are lectures, on every variety of subject, given outside our own building in the evenings – two or three a week – debates, sing-songs and so on.

We play Poker or Bridge most nights out on our verandah, between roll-call and lights-out (I belonging to the former school). We get a game of cricket about once a week and although I have never been very keen on the game, it is quite amusing and gives one an enjoyable afternoon's outing down near the sea – a welcome break from the usual surroundings. One or two Plays have also been put on up here and proved very successful considering the difficulties over clothes and scenery etc.

Daily routine

Perhaps I might try and give you some idea of the normal daily routine. We are on Japanese time – one and a half hours in advance of normal (clocks on 1½ hours) so we don't wake up in the morning till about 8 o'clock or later; early morning tea at 9 (minus sugar and milk) and breakfast at 10.30.

One is as likely as not to be on some form of fatigue before breakfast, such as drawing rations, firewood, or cutting up vegetables in the cook house. Personally have just taken over wood-sawing, a permanent daily fatigue from 8.15 until 10 (with 15 minutes break for tea) and at any other time of the day if and when required. This absolves me from all the normal general fatigues like those mentioned above and helps keep the muscles in shape. Breakfast is always "porridge" (rice made to look like same) and sweetened coconut milk, with probably a slice of bread or a chapatti. Our other meals are rice – main bulk – with the small addition of some form of curry, stew, fish-cake or rissole. (The Japs give us a fresh vegetable ration and fresh or frozen meat twice a week – and the Mess subscriptions enable us to supplement the meals with a few tins of fish or bully-beef, etc.)

Lunch is at 2 p.m.

I suppose the majority of us spend the morning reading. The little library is far too small for the multitude but one can still find some quite good stuff in it; we hope to do a change over of books with another area in the near future. But reading is not the only occupation; many of us have been making a dab at foreign languages, with quite promising results. I myself have been learning German for the last four months or so – 3 till 4 p.m. every Monday, Tuesday and Friday, with homework to be done in between. Our balcony alone produces some pretty remarkable noises when we all get down to it together, one of us talking Spanish, another Urdu and a third Chinese. It is the latter which causes all the trouble.

I have also just induced a misguided fellow to try and teach me the clarinet, so that will occupy an hour or so every morning.

Sketches of the Japanese by the artist Ronald Searle, a fellow prisoner of war at Changi

After lunch till about 4.30 is a sleep period, when the art-and-craft minded are asked to still their sawings and hammerings.

The really strong-minded succeed in saving over their lunchtime slice of bread or chapatti to eat at 4.30 with the tea that comes over from the cook house.

Dinner is usually at 7.15 p.m., before which the time is usually filled by more reading, Bridge or an evening stroll inside the wire – and a shower-bath just down the hill.

After dinner there is a general exodus out to the front terrace to gossip on the day's rumours and to watch the sun set over the Johore Straits – often very fine indeed. It is at this time of day that time seems to hang heaviest and one's thoughts automatically turn to better times and places – to those at home, wondering what they are doing and thinking ...

Back to the room at 9 o'clock when we probably settle down to a game of Poker by the yellow, fitful light of a small oil lamp. Occasionally a total blackout is ordered and then indeed it is a long and tedious evening – especially if one has no cigarettes! Lights out 10.45 – which also means no more talking or noise (just like School again!) – and so to bed.

Monday 3 August

Another week gone by. I had a large back tooth yanked out on Thursday by the dentist over in Southern Area – an excellent piece of work – felt literally nothing.

That was my fourth visit to him and I have another appointment tomorrow for a small filling. There was a bumper crop of Canteen Stores last week; we had foolishly ordered far above our incomes and unfortunately it all arrived – honey, treacle, razor blades, sauces, etc. – with the result that some of us were flung violently into debt – myself to the tune of 5 dollars. Fortunately I am gradually managing to sell a few of the luxuries such as the honey but even so I shall be in debt until the pay-day after next. Hence no cigarettes!

Yesterday was quite a typical Sunday. Lay in till 9 in the morning, feeling far too sleepy for the Holy Communion at 8.30 (held every Sunday in the dining room).

Half an hour's sawing at 9.30 and about an hour more after breakfast, in the broiling sun, to make up for what we missed in the early morning.

After cooling down and bathing it was almost time for lunch – at 1.30 on Sundays – this time quite a good hot vegetable curry. Read and slept in the afternoon – then an excellent piece of jam roly-poly for tea (which we should have had for lunch but which wasn't ready in time).

Took the Clarinet down to my usual tree for an hour's practice before dinner and got so engrossed that I had no time for a bath.

Attended the usual evening Service out in the front of the building at 7.45 – another very good talk from the A.C.G.

Into the dining room at 9 o'clock to listen to Beethoven's 3rd Symphony on the gramophone. We have these gramophone concerts every Sunday evening and extraordinarily pleasant it is to sit there in the dark and get carried completely out of the present for an hour and a half or so – armed with a packet of Chinese cigarettes.

Sunday 9 August

It has been a good week for entertainment. The evening lectures included a talk by the G.O.C. on the Norway Campaign – one on the Australian Surf Clubs (when the lecturer likened the thrill of surfing to skiing) – and an excellent talk on Test Cricket by Barnett, the Australian Test player, now a common P.O.W. down with the rest of the A.I.F. contingent.

On Friday the Australian concert party came up and gave us another of their performances; and last night was the pièce de resistance – A.A. Milne's 'Dover Road', put on at the theatre over in 18 Div. area. Most of us were agreed that we had seldom, if ever, seen a better amateur show, even disregarding the fact that we are in a P.O.W. Camp with all the obvious difficulties in production. It was a really excellent show, perfect down to the last detail – a bell in the interval 3 minutes before the curtain – the orchestra – the clothes, both male and female – the stage furniture and effects – and, of course, A1 acting. It was an evening that will stand out in my memory for many months to come, so much did it lift us clean out of Changi Camp.

Either tomorrow or the day after, a party comprising all officers in the camp of the rank of Colonel and above and the Sappers from our building are scheduled to be sailing for Japan. But they have been standing by for nearly three weeks now; their departure has already been postponed twice, so it won't surprise me at all if it falls through a third time.

There is talk of more of us having to go before long – either to Japan or to a large camp built for 10,000 in Saigon.

As one cannot possibly predict what the future may hold in store, I feel that I don't really mind either way – whether I go or stay; it might be quite a good plan to see the world at someone else's expense.

We could see two quite large vessels on the southern horizon this morning – coming in towards Keppel Harbour – said to be the S.S. Conte Verde and Asama Mar on their return from Lorenzo Marques, where it was sincerely hoped they had taken our postcards, for onward despatch; and also all our names to India. I don't seem to have mentioned those postcards before; it was on June 20th that we wrote them, only being allowed to write the very shortest message to say that we were still alive and kicking. I only hope to God they do eventually fetch up at their destinations and so alleviate the awful doubt that must, I know, exist in the minds of so many at home and all over the world. It is probably too much to hope that these boats have brought us any mail – but you never know (and possibly a few thousand cases of sausages and beer?!).

The perfect weather continues with its brilliant sun and light breezes occasionally a little too hot – and a tropical cloudburst every ten days or so. The sun has no effect on us now, of course, we are all tanned to a luscious chocolate shade that I'm sure the girls would love; we never wear a shirt, except during meals, or a hat, even when out playing cricket through the heat of the afternoon. Which reminds me that we, as a Regt., are playing the Gordons tomorrow and I am at last fitted out with a pair of P.T. shoes; got a brand new pair this morning for a dollar, off a Sapper due for Japan and who wanted to convert his shoes into food!

Sunday 16 August

Time marches on ... Six months ago yesterday since the Capitulation, and six months tomorrow that we entered Changi Camp. A good chunk of time to have put behind us, though possibly but a small proportion of the whole.

I consider it quite a good omen that the Japs celebrated yesterday as what they call Malaya Independence Day – do they think they cannot afford to wait a year for an anniversary celebration? I hope so. But there's probably no grounds for such hopes.

Quite an eventful day yesterday. It was arranged that eighteen of us (from this Brigade) should form the fatigue party to push the cart for one of the Camp 'local purchase' officers – a job normally allotted to B.O.R.s from other areas. We breakfasted early – 8.15 – and were over to the Supply Depot by 9.

Collected our cart there (denuded chassis of a lorry) and connected up with our local purchase officers and we were away. We followed the main road into Singapore until we reached the huge Civil gaol – still inside the main Camp area – where all the civil P.O.W.s are collected, including some 150 women and children.

There we took on our Jap guard from the Camp. Followed the road about a couple of miles, then up left into a small Chinese Kampong where we found huge piles of pineapples and about a dozen crates of eggs (hen's and duck's) all set out ready for us to take back to the Camp. The purchasing officers having done their bargaining, we loaded up and the Jap then allowed us to go and take our fill from the numerous little food stalls all round – a fully organised young market set up by the Chinese to cater for the working parties visiting this particular area for local purchase – the whole place swarming with chattering chinks – men, women and children – mostly children, an attractive lot as they always are – and all in seemingly quite good spirits.

It started to rain, so an excellent party ensued in the Coffee Shop where we proceeded to gorge on all the numerous 'eats' – very appetising and needless to say, not a grain of rice to be seen anywhere – and really excellently made coffee for 6 cents a cup, which most of us had in preference to beer.

Fortunately we had received our Amenity Pay the day before so I was able to bust a whole 43 cents – a vast extravagance for one day but it was

Pulling the rations fatigue cart

well worth it, to feel one's stomach really distended again! Our Jap guard, incidentally, also joined the party – drank his beer and pressed cigarettes on those at his table – an odd party.

Our eggs proved quite a heavy load on the return journey but on the down-hill stretches we all piled on board and free-wheeled as far as we could. We were back for a 2 p.m. lunch, having had a most excellent morning. I had a small accident just before arriving home; it was whilst I was in the act of jumping onto the truck that I caught my foot between the rear wheel and the road and wrenched my ankle and instep quite severely. (It didn't give me much sleep last night – still very swollen and slightly painful today; am having it X-rayed tomorrow.)

In the evening the nucleus of the Southern Area Review came up and put over quite an entertaining little show. This morning – at long last – Party 'A' of the lot going to Japan actually left the camp for Singapore, thus draining our building of about 150 people. Party 'B' are due to go on Tuesday.

As a result of the exodus we have come by some of the beds and other furniture left behind. In fact the whole morning, while I have been writing, has been made hideous by hammerings and scrapings, and heated arguments amongst those reorganising their homes.

The long drought seems to have broken – wet and overcast yesterday and again today; and last night I actually had to put a blanket over me for the first time since we've been here.

Monday 24 August

Many thanks, South Africa – A very welcome present, last week, from the South African Govt. in the shape of maize flour, jam (over 1lb per head), sweets and soup powder – all sent to us through the International Red X. Let's hope they remember us again at Christmas time.

But if that can happen, then why not mail? Surely it would be the simplest matter; presumably the Japs won't allow it.

We have just completed a general change round of quarters, following on the departure of the Sappers. We now have our own Brigade dining-room – the original Mess billiard room – and are independent of the other Brigades with whom we shared the same room before, and was the cause of much petty friction over meal times, stealing of communal plates, etc .

We have also moved rooms – ourselves and our original neighbours – and have taken over the large, airy ante room in the main part of the building; infinitely more room than we had before and an excellent large verandah looking north over the Johore Straits. I sincerely hope we won't have to move anywhere else yet awhile as we are very well off now and are quite 'house proud'.

Quite a few of us were interviewed by the Japanese, the other day, on various places in India to which we had been and about which they wanted information. I was down for Chittagong and told the Interpreter all I could remember about the type of country, the roads, rivers, etc., in answer to his questions. The two Japs were very polite and even apologised to me for having me along when I had a swollen ankle (which incidentally is almost O.K. again).

The Japs had up all those hailing from Ceylon for interrogation about a couple of months ago.

Went over to an excellent Classical Concert last night, in Southern Area, the second half of the programme being Beethoven's Violin Concerto in 'D' (just a violin and piano); the violinist – Dennis East – played in the London Philharmonic before joining up and is really top-notch class.

Off now to wash some clothes – at which we are becoming quite proficient – and then, I hear, some South African soup for lunch.

Monday 26 October

There seems to have been rather a long lapse since I last contributed to these sheets but a succession of hectic events put me out of stride and I was too idle to resume . The memorable 'Selerang Incident' took place in the first week of September: the story very briefly was this ...

The Japanese intimated to our O.C. troops that they wished every P. of W. individually to sign a proforma to the effect that he promised that he would not, under any circumstances, attempt to escape. This everyone naturally enough refused to do, whereupon the Japs, very much annoyed, proceeded to apply their own measures for ensuring they got what they wanted.

Shortly before lunch on Wednesday, 2nd September, we in our Bde. were told that we must remove ourselves, bag and baggage, to Serlang Square – about 2½ miles away from the A.I.F. Area – and that the move must be completed by 6pm that evening.

All other areas were ordered to move to the same rendezvous. No transport was provided and it was obvious that we had to take our complete cookhouse and all rations.

Thus commenced a truly remarkable trek – every P. of W. in the camp converging on one small barrack area, carrying, by all improvised means imaginable, everything from his bed to his toothbrush and any small items of necessary furniture which could be squeezed onto the top-heavy handcarts. We all did as many trips as we could during the time available and by about 5.30 p.m. the move was completed.

Try and imagine, then, the picture at Selerang Square – just over 19,000 men herded like animals into an area roughly 300×200 yds., surrounded by seven three-storied barrack blocks – a barrack area normally intended for one full-strength battalion in peace. A road runs round the area just outside the buildings and no man was allowed over this road (machine gun positions were set at all four corners of the area).

The barracks themselves could only house a proportion of the multitude and the square was therefore a seething mass of humanity, sorting out kit and hastily rigging up scratch cookhouses, where space allowed, to prepare the evening meal. The very centre of the square was left as free as possible

The 'Selerang Incident': the crowded Selerang Barracks

41

and was devoted to the digging of latrine-pits. My own unit was fortunate in being allotted some space on a ground floor; our total indoor space for 18 Officers was a strip of floor 28 feet long by 3 feet wide, though about four of us managed to find enough room to sleep outside.

To cut a long story short, after sticking it out for three days, with the troops in remarkably good spirits, it became obvious that if we lived under those conditions any longer, with sanitary conditions as they were, we would very soon start dying off like flies (there already being Diphtheria and Dysentery in the Camp). Consequently O.C. Troops issued a written order for all men to sign the required oath, on account of the extreme duress and on the morning of the 5th we all trekked back to our respective homes – having had an experience which none of us, I am sure, will ever forget.

But the Japanese had had their eye on our Temple Hill building for quite a long time, as being too good a spot for P.O.W.s and they also wanted to turn out prisoners from all barracks directly overlooking the sea or Johore Straits.

So on Sept. 8th we finally evacuated Temple Hill and took up our new abode in one of the end barracks of Selerang Square – the scene of our incarceration three days back. Most of us regretted having to go at the time but one soon gets used to anything these days and this area has quite a few advantages over Temple Hill. For one thing, we have much more country to wander about in – the whole A.I.F. area and II Div. only just over the main road. And a football ground just outside our barrack.

We are about as well off for bed space as we were in our new room in Temple Hill, with a good wide verandah running the length of the building – and on the top story, with a good breath of air, we have a view over to the gaol, only about 2 miles away and also get a glimpse of normal native life outside the camp – screams of children playing by a Malay school just over to the right.

Then there is the Australian Canteen only five minutes walk away – a well run show and adequately stocked; I find it difficult not to make a daily visit and fritter away my odd cents on peanuts, eggs, bananas and peanut-brittle, etc.

Finances

Perhaps the chief event since we have been in this area has been that of pay. The Japanese have decided to pay Officers on a proper basis (while B.O.R.s still only get their Amenity Grant, as before). Our first payment was for September, which we received late, not until 15th October, there having been a first-class muddle over nominal role and strengths.

The details of payment, to take for example my own case, as a Captain, are as follows: Basic pay 122.50; less deductions by I.J.A. for lodging, food and clothing 60; less deductions by Comdr P.O.W. for Hospital and 'Vitamins' 10; banked by I.J.A. in Singapore 32.50. Balance Cash 20.

It has been worked so that all Officers of the rank of Lieutenant and above get this net balance of 20 dollars, whilst the unfortunate 2/Lts., of whom there are a great number, only have a balance of 10.83. Consequently in our unit we have equalised pay so that we all have a round 15 dollars. 2.50 of that goes into the Mess and 50c for a sports fund, so that we each have about 13 dollars a month to play with; – hardly a fortune but we are infinitely richer men than when we were only seeing a bare 5 dollars Amenity Grant.

Red Cross

Then there have been the magnificent efforts of the Red Cross from South Africa. During the course of the last month or so we have received two separate individual allotments, including Virginian cigarettes (60 per man), sugar, sweet biscuits, bully-beef, jam, tinned milk, etc., and also other things which we put into the cookhouse, such as cocoa (which we now have three times a week in the evenings), soup, dhal, tinned meat and veg., and so on – with the result that our standard of messing has gone up enormously. Quite a few lucky individuals received Red X parcels containing a marvellous assortment of clothing and toilet nick-nacks – sent by their wives and relations in S. Africa.

There is talk of more Red X ships arriving in the very near future. So there are Great Expectations of similar parcels arriving from England and India ... Also rumours of real mail – letters and postcards – but I personally think that's too much to hope for ...

... anyway, I can't help thinking that a letter after all these months would be most unsettling to the mind ...

New arrivals

We have recently received some interesting new arrivals into Changi. First, a large party who had been prisoners over in Java – mostly Australians and some British Gunners. One of these Aussies gave a lecture one evening, telling us all about his experiences in Timor, the Jap attack, the fighting and their eventual capture.

Then there was the arrival of a few fellows from Kuala Lumpur, the P.O.W. camp there having been broken up. Two or three were Officers of our own Bde., and were able to fill the gaps in the story of Slim River and other such places where they were captured.

Those from K.L. who didn't come down here were evidently sent up to Bangkok.

The most recent arrivals were a party of Yanks over from Java – containing, amongst others, a Texas Field Regt. and U.S. Navy personnel. This resulted, the other night, in probably the most interesting and amusing lecture that we have yet had, by an American Naval Lt.Comdr. who was a survivor from the S.S. Houston – delivered with a delightful broad New York twang and oozing with ripe Yank humour from start to finish – a very refreshing evening.

Last night, talking of lectures, a Colonel who got away by ship from Singapore on the night of the 12/13th Febuary, gave us a vivid account of his experiences, trying to get across to Sumatra. It made a very sorry tale indeed, hearing, at the end, the names of all the get-away boats which were either sunk or captured, some of them before they had gone any distance at all; and the names of people known to have been on those boats.

Everyday life here is much the same as it was over on Temple Hill. My German class is still going strong, four days a week. I came off wood-sawing and took my turn as table-waiter for a fortnight – quite an energetic job as we had no less than four people all sick-in-quarters at the same time (fever & tummy), involving two or three trips upstairs every meal with their special light diet from the cookhouse.

The Aussies here run a non-stop concert in their new entertainment hall (specially constructed stage, etc.), with a change of programme every fortnight or so. We went along the other night; the star performer was a professional actor, who, incidentally, took the lead in the filming of 'Charley's Aunt' a few years back.

The Australians' Convalescent Depot is another centre of amusement. The building is the old Gordons Officers Mess and has had electric light laid on for quite a long time; they give gramophone concerts on a radiogram (less radio) most Saturday nights – and also a full sized billiard table and ping-pong, with electric fans going, etc. – all very civilised.

The Japs are going to put all these buildings onto the electric main before long, so they say but I don't expect for one moment to see it before Christmas.

As it is now, all our Kerosine oil has run out and candles are unobtainable at the Canteen – so the evening hours of darkness are rather trying.

Sunday 8 November

Last week saw a most regrettable split in our Brigade. News first came in that all the Officers of III Corps. as well as most of the B.O.R.s had orders to move up-country, together with parties from Div. and that we must be ready to move within three days. So we accordingly set about collecting our kit together and making up deficiencies and so on; the move was scheduled to be to Bangkok where a large P.O.W. camp is said to have been built.

Next day, however, it evolved that not quite all the Officers would be going: all Corps Sigs, 4 Bde. and 8 Bde. were to go in toto, and enough from our own Bde. (about half) to make up the required number laid down by the Japs. So off they all went on Wednesday last – the 8th; we saw them all off early in the morning, packed about 40 to a 3-ton lorry. Our unit was not chosen to go but we very unfortunately lost two of our Volunteers who were standing by as reserves for III Corps and had suddenly to go at the very last moment.

Life just now feels very flat with all those fellows gone. In many ways I wish we had accompanied them but possibly the best rule to work on here is to let Fate take its own course.

The original Japan Party has been warned to stand by again and there is also talk about further moves up country. As for ourselves (the remainder of 28 Bde.), we might either go up country or be moved over into 11 Div. Area – no one knows, as usual, and life is full of rumours and counter-rumours.

Meanwhile there has been an enormous influx of Dutch and Javanese native troops into the area of our barrack square. They are indeed a varied selection, ranging from well educated English-speaking Dutch Officers down to the very blackest Javanese imaginable.

A surprising number of them speak English; they say they find it undoubtedly the easiest language that they learn when at school.

My German teacher, incidentally, went up with the Bangkok party and the prospects of finding anyone else don't look very rosy; a great pity as we had reached a stage when it was becoming increasingly interesting and rewarding.

One of our Volunteers actually received a letter last week from his wife in South Africa – a truly memorable event. A bit of mail evidently came in on the Red X ships but the Japs have only distributed a total of about 150 letters in the whole camp. His wife wrote purely on chance, none of them over in S. Africa having had any news of us whatsoever.

Sunday 29 November

Since last writing I have been leading a very strenuous existence with little or no time to myself and today, being our first 'whole holiday' is the first real opportunity I have had of writing up the story.

On Monday 9th Nov. Alec Ogilvie and I left the Brigade and came over to join the Japanese Gardens Unit, which I shall explain. We joined the unit for various reasons (not enough space to mention here) but it suffices to say that we shall probably be among the very last of the P.O.W.s to be moved from Singapore Island. The Japanese started this extensive gardens scheme over two months ago, the idea being to produce vegetable gardens capable of supplying the needs of the whole camp.

Each of the four Areas of the camp runs its own garden area – the organising staffs being all grouped together as one independent unit – strength about 13 Officers and 70 O.R.s.

We are fortunately still quartered in the A.I.F. Area, just by the main road leading into Singapore and so still see quite a lot of the fellows in the Battalion and occasionally go over for the odd meal or cocoa in the evenings.

Alec works in the 11 Div. part of the garden whilst I am helping out Vander Gucht (a planter from this country) with the Southern Area garden.

The whole concern is run – remarkable to say – by a Japanese corporal – Fukuda by name – who has under him four area supervisors, all young Korean privates (agriculturalists in their own country).

Our own Southern Area boss is Yamamoto, an energetic little man and sometimes very trying to deal with, especially when things are not going exactly according to his directions; he speaks no English at all except for the odd 'begin work' and 'come here' which we unfortunately taught him.

We have an interpreter living with us in the Mess who spends his entire day at the beck and call of Fukuda and visiting each garden area in turn to help us out of our difficulties.

Owing to the gardens still being almost in their infancy, the hours of work are very long; we breakfast at 8.15 (same old inevitable rice porridge) and at about 9 we hear the tramp of our working parties arriving outside on the road. We dish them out with their tools and go on down to the gardens, only about a mile distant, this side of the gaol. All the working parties, incidentally, are provided by the parties arrived over from Java; in the case of Southern Area they consist of Dutch, Americans and Australians, in varying proportions each day and totalling about 400 men daily.

The work, up to date, has consisted almost entirely of clearing the ground of subterranean stumps and tree trunks, many of them of great age and fantastic shapes and sizes. There is a break from 12.30 till 1.30 for lunch which for everyone is brought down and eaten at the gardens.

Work goes on till 5 p.m. when all parties pack up and go home. We get back to the Mess at about 5.30 or after, and there's just time for a cup of tea and a bath before supper at 6.15. A long and tiring day.

Originally work was to be seven full days a week but we protested strongly and the arrangement now is that we get two half days a week – Wednesday and Sunday. Last Wednesday had to be a full day owing to 29,000 'Kladi' roots arriving on Tuesday evening, for planting immediately, so today we were given the whole day off.

We put about 8,000 of these Kladi (a type of Yam) into the cleared part of our own garden and there is now a vast difference in the look of the area since when I joined the show.

Sunday 20 December

Over a year ago, now, since we left IPOH and went up north to meet the Japs and over ten months since we became prisoners – quite a reasonable hunk of time to have put behind us. Meanwhile work on the gardens has been forging steadily ahead; about half the area of my own garden area is planted now (peanuts, onions, spinach and Chinese radish and lettuce) and it all really does look quite impressive. I see I didn't explain, when writing before, the nature of my work on the garden; I am number two to Vander Gucht and we run the planning and planting under the orders of Fukuda (since promoted sergeant, by the way) and young Yamomoto.

The various working parties come down under their own officers and we set them their various tasks for the day and see that they go about it the right way, etc. – in fact strolling round all day, supervising the work.

In many ways it is a difficult position to be in, requiring a great deal of tact; we naturally cannot give them an 'order' to do any particular piece of work, as it is the Japanese they are working for – not us.

And for that same reason it is sometimes difficult to keep everyone from slacking off and only making a pretence of work when the Japanese are near, watching them.

We had a bit of trouble the other day when an American sergeant sloshed a sergeant-major on our Staff over the chin and hurt him quite badly – the American objected strongly to being given an order by the British. There seems to be a definite anti-British feeling amongst some of them, probably bound up with an inferiority complex. But since the regrettable incident occurred, the Yanks have been extremely pleasant and have been working excellently.

There's been a great deal of rain lately, with one particularly heavy spell when 16 inches fell in 41 days. The garden became a Lake, footbridges were carried away and general havoc was wrought. But we have since cleared up the mess and the garden is none the worse. It's the north-east monsoon period (during which it was generally supposed that the Japanese would find it quite impossible to make a landing on the east coast of Malaya!) and the rains continue until about the end of January.

Another overseas party went off about three weeks ago which included Gen. Heath (Comdr. 111 Corps) whom we were all very sorry to lose. We gave him quite a good send off, with the concert party Band in attendance and 'Old Lang Syne', etc. A new Japanese General has taken over as O.C. P.O.W. Camp, and his first move has been to return all our working parties from Singapore, about ten thousand men in all. Six thousand are coming into the A.I.F. area so even we, in our select little unit, have had to push in a bit tighter; Alec and I spent our time this afternoon (a half-holiday) moving into the next-door building, where the other officers are; we are now five of us in a room decidedly smaller than our previous one but nevertheless we are not at all badly off. The remainder of III Corps, including our own fellows from 28 Bde. have all moved over to III Div. Area and are very closely packed indeed.

Monday 21 December

Rather an exhausting day. A bit of trouble with the Javanese Dutch; one party of them whom I had out grass cutting took the whole afternoon to do a small job of work which need only have taken 45 minutes at the outside. It appears they have got it into their heads that they are going to be moved overseas or up-country in the near future and are consequently tending to 'pack up' in their work on the gardens. A party of about eleven hundred Javanese troops left yesterday (presumed for overseas), so perhaps it is, in fact, the commencement of evacuation on a large scale.

Saw a lot of Aussie troops marching in from Singapore today and convoys of vehicles with their kit. They say that each of the large barrack buildings in Selerang Square will have to house about 750 men – pretty uncomfortable living.

We have been seeing some excellent shows put on by the A.I.F. Concert Party, changing every fortnight. I heard them today practising for their special Christmas show. I believe at one time they thought of putting on a Christmas pantomime, in the hopes of getting the children over from the gaol; the idea was also to run a sports gymkhana for them on the 11 Div. padang. The Japanese have been urgently requested, twice, to fall in with these ideas but the latest news is that they are regarding the project very unfavourably. Anyway, their final decision has not yet been given so there is yet hope. It would be wonderful to see some English kids again.

But even if that fails to come off, people all over the camp have been busy for the past two months making toys for them – we saw an exhibition of them the other night at the Convalescent Depot and there is a truly marvellous selection of stuff – much of it really talented work – so I hope that Christmas won't be a completely negative affair for those kids over in the gaol, as it otherwise might have been. I may say that we have been giving not a little thought to our own Christmas programme.

Needless to say that means FOOD. Our Mess Secretary assures us that he can fix up scrambled eggs on toast for breakfast and other equally fantastic dishes for lunch and supper – so we have great hopes.

Incidentally we have been feeding quite well in this Mess and one's mind doesn't dwell nearly so much on food as it used to in earlier days. I suppose our stomachs have learned to get all they can out of rice – most people are weighing very little below normal.

I, for one, am almost exactly the same weight as I was in peace time.

Sunday 27 December

Christmas came and went. Very short and sweet – in fact it already feels a month old in my memory, now that we have had two days of the normal routine.

No Christmas could have been more lacking in everything that normally goes to make it the great occasion that it is – except, in spirit, which was miraculously very much to the fore. There seemed to be a general spirit of remarkable cheerfulness and optimism and everyone genuinely believing that it would be their only Christmas in such straits.

Xmas Eve was a normal full day on the gardens; some of us went to a special Carol Service in the evening at St. Andrew's Chapel – very well put on indeed but unfortunately the singing was by the Choir only except for the first and last hymns.

The Great Day itself was, naturally enough, a whole holiday from the gardens.

First big event was breakfast – 9.30: Mabela porridge, scrambled eggs on toast and fresh grilled fish – enough to start off any P.O.W. with the festive spirit. Church service at St. Andrews (this time the congregation were allowed to let themselves go) after which Alec and I went over to pay the Bn. a visit in III Div. Area.

Lunch: roast chicken (got from the Chinese) and vegetables, followed by a very creditable effort at plum pudding, made out of dates, raisins, peanuts etc., with the table lavishly strewn with more dates, sweets, cheroots and so on, (stomach already feeling laden by now). P.M. (for myself) – bed, book and sleep, waking at 5.30pm – although there were such attractions as athletic meetings and football going on, with bands playing and all that sort of thing, (Mad dogs and Englishmen ...!) Supper was a cold repast, served and washed up by ourselves so as to give the cookhouse staff a holiday: cold bully-beef and potatoes – tinned guavas and chocolate sauce – ably assisted down by a spot of 'Samsu', the local Chinese 'Hooch' – enough for us to toast absent friends and leave the table with the right taste in our mouths.

Followed quite an amusing evening of sing-song out on the lawn, helped along by one of the party plucking at a guitar – and so to bed. A very successful day. I wonder what it was like in old England ... ?

A full day's work yesterday Boxing Day – but a diversion in the evening in the shape of a concert in the A.I.F. concert hall – full orchestral pieces and vocal and instrumental solos; a very creditable show considering that, to get a balanced orchestra, they have had to alter the Key of two clarinets by stuffing paper into odd holes in the instruments – use ordinary signal wire in the violins (the proper strings being unobtainable) – and employ various other makeshifts.

About 3,000 more men back from Singapore today – some marching, some in transport; convoys of kit lorries coming in throughout the day. It was a most exhausting day, physically – rained in the early morning and remained hot and steamy until evening. The sort of weather that would gradually get one down; I often feel I should like to go out into an icy cold mountain blizzard and have icicles dangling from my eyelashes instead of sweat.

1943

Monday 4 January

At last the time has arrived when we no longer have to talk about next year with regard to getting out of this damned place (at least we hope so!). There wasn't much incentive for merry-making on New Year's Eve so we all went to our beds at the usual time but a large section of the community evidently thought they had better do something about it, for at midnight and after, there were ringings of bells, bashing of tins and parties of songsters all round the place droning out 'Old Lang Syne' etc. – until they all thought better of it and we got some sleep.

New Year's Day is fortunately one of the biggest days on the Japanese calendar, so we had a whole holiday off the garden. Alec and I went over to lunch with the boys in 28 Bde. – stayed over there for an afternoon sleep and watched some of them play rugger against the Australians in the evening.

The Japs made an issue of wine to the whole camp, on the scale of a bottle to every ten men; Heaven knows what it was – strongly resembled methylated spirit – and pretty potent. Nevertheless it was a nice gesture on the Jap's part.

On Saturday night we went over to see the new concert party show – a topical version of 'Cinderella' – brilliantly clever. It had been specially laid on in the hopes of getting the kids over from the gaol but that scheme never came off.

Incidentally I had occasion to take some men over to the gaol football ground last week, to collect some grass and I managed to have a word or two with the civilian fellows living in the gaol, who were out working on their own gardens. They evidently had quite a good Xmas over there and they were particularly grateful for the toys which had been sent over for the kids. On Xmas Day all those possessing wives or other female relations in the gaol were allowed over to see them for about 45 minutes or so.

Yesterday evening, Sunday, 28 Bde. threw an evening supper party to members of the Aussie concert party, who went over complete with squeeze-box, guitar, etc., and gave us a couple of hours of first class impromptu entertainment – with cocoa, biscuits and tinned pineapple liberally supplied by 28 Bde.

A full, long, hot day down on the gardens today – everything going along quite well. We shall be parting with our American gang from tomorrow onwards; they will be going to work on another area. Possibly just as well as they are still a potential source or trouble. Today a Jap found two of them picking the 'forbidden fruit' off a rambutan tree in the orchard, when they should have been working. They were made to stand to attention in the sun for 3 hours and miss their lunch.

Tuesday 12 January

Nothing much of interest to report. Been having a spot of drought – not a drop of rain during the past ten days or so and quite a strong wind blowing; watering the gardens is becoming a major problem.

Food is steadily on the downgrade these days. We ran out of all Red X tinned food a fortnight or so ago and no bully-beef, etc., is obtainable at the canteen; also the fresh meat issue ceased nearly a month ago – so we are living entirely on rice and vegetables, with a very occasional issue of fish.

Fortunately one can still buy peanuts and dates, etc., at the canteen, which help to fill in the gaps. But it is becoming quite a problem on the garden, with regard to the long hours of work: the average man just hasn't got it in him (literally!) to do much in the way of work after about 3.30 or 4 p.m.

We have stated the case in strong terms to the Japanese but so far with no result. We, incidentally, are paying $7.50 a month towards our messing whereas the Dutch and Javanese are paid so little that they can only contribute about 1 dollar each. Once again there are great movements going on, both in and out of the Camp.

A party of 3,000 Dutch, Javanese and Australians arrived from Java five days ago and similar parties are leaving almost every day – some by ship and some by train, up country (probably to Bangkok).

All the Yanks went in the first party.

I attended a series of five talks last week at the 'Con. Depot', on the subject of the setting up of a great 'New Order', based, of course, on the moral uplift of mankind (the old theme) – all the speakers were excellent and the whole enterprise proved surprisingly popular – crowded hall each night and heated questions and answers at the termination of each lecture. It certainly did a lot to get chaps thinking on intelligent lines. Following on the lectures, study circles are being started, to discuss all the different aspects of like in general (social, economic, international relations, Christian unity, etc.) – and the hope is that Changi will eventually be able to put forward some useful constructive suggestions for world betterment.

Monday 18 January

Another spate of lectures last week. Went to hear John Stephens talking on the North West Frontier (of India) and on the next night on Gurkhas. He had given both lectures much thought and preparation and they were excellent.

It never ceases to surprise and amaze me what a legendary name the Gurkha has amongst Australian troops (and British, for that matter); hardly a day goes by without my hearing them mentioned in one way or another, or being asked questions as to whether they do this and that. Incidentally, we had our first contact with the Bn. a couple of days ago, when a few men of our own and of the 2/9th came in on the ration lorries from Singapore to the base supply depot.

An officer of the 2/1st G. happened to be there and talked with one of our Havildars who asked after me. We are hoping any day for them to come in again.

No afternoon sleep on either of our last two half days – had to play football over in 11 Div; far too energetic on our scanty rations but I must admit I feel all the better for it.

Thursday 21 January

Quite a number of lucky individuals have received letters and wireless messages lately, from England, India and elsewhere – they make one mad with envy. A fellow in 9 GR had a message from his wife in India to the effect that he had recently become the father of twin sons – and another bloke on the garden the other day had the nerve to go about waving in people's faces no less than six letters which he had received – all on the same day. It looks as if our folks are trying hard to communicate with us but that only a very few have discovered the correct way of going about it – or it may all be purely a matter of luck.

More moves of Java parties going on almost daily now, both in and out of the camp, in many ways I feel quite envious of them, pouring out of the camp in their lorries, as we wave them farewell from the garden. It's over eleven months now and I, for one, have only once been beyond the gaol (and then only a couple of miles). I'm trying hard to work a trip into Singapore – anything for a change from the daily routine of the gardens and our quarters. The officers of this unit have started giving lectures to the other ranks every Monday and Friday evening; they are proving very popular. I may get up and natter about skiing reminiscences – (if I discover there is any enthusiasm for the subject).

Wonderful moonlit nights now – liable to fill one's mind with many wandering, fanciful thoughts – strongly to be deprecated.

Wednesday 17 February

Got rather behind with this screed, due mainly to having been occupied every evening with one of these modern 900-page novels – 'The Sun is my Undoing' by Marguerite Steen – very excellent indeed.

About three weeks ago all Dutch and Javanese ceased coming out to work on the gardens (by order of the Japs) and all labour has been British and Australian. At about the same time, also, I broke away from the Southern Area garden and took over a new garden area – (quite a small plot of cleared rubber, 4 acres, rather apart from the main area known as the 'Blue House', owing to there being there an old disused Chinese house.

I have a W.O. and one O.R. to help me and we have about 50–70 chaps working there. We have very little attention from the Japanese; there is one little Korean detailed to the area but he never makes his presence felt and is, in fact, quite a pleasant fellow. The plan is to plant up the whole area with sweet potatoes, so we have been going ahead with bed-making as quickly as possible. We have already got 12 blocks of beds planted out, about 8 of which we put in last Sunday morning when the Japs suddenly produced an enormous quantity of cuttings; we got about 90 men down to planting and managed to get them all in by lunch time and so still got our half day.

During the week previous to that we had 2 days of continuous heavy rain – nearly as much as the downpour three or four months back. Fortunately the drainage coped with it pretty well and our area is already nearly back to normal (one corner still too wet to do anything with at present).

This week a new garden unit area is being formed, whereby all personnel working on the gardens will become permanent parties; all those from 18 Div. and Southern Area are coming up into 11 Div. area, just over the road, and the Australians will stay where they are in the A.I.F. area. And I hear that 11 Div. area will then be called the "Gardens and Wood" area. That, of course, means that our 28 Bde. chaps have to get out of it and they are all moving down into Southern Area, near to where we originally started life, in Temple Hill.

2 GR gave an excellent farewell party last Sunday night, to which Alec and I went. Some of the A.I.F. concert party also went over to help make it a party. Just exactly a year ago today that we marched in from Singapore, having parted with our men in the morning. Can't help feeling that we must have crossed the half-way line. Almost a touch of home the other day when three of our N.C.O.s got letters from England and one of them from Aldershot.

Mail keeps on slowly filtering out from the Jap. H.Q. so I haven't given up hope yet, they evidently censor so many a week. Incidentally, the Japs have given sanction to the A.I.F. to send messages to Australia, some of which have already gone, so the hope is they may extend arrangements for England and India.

February 1943

Operation Longcloth was a morale boost for Allied troops in Burma when the 'Chindits" had a number of successes attacking the infrastructure behind Japanese lines.

Thursday 25 February

I am taking a whole day off from the gardens today and finding it quite difficult to know how to fill up the day. Since the formation of the garden unit, a few days ago, we have got a few Volunteers (from the Malaya Volunteer Force, etc.) helping us out; they are mostly ex-rubber planters and know all about things agricultural, so some of us have started taking one full day off per week, over and above the two half holidays.

Yesterday, being Wednesday and a half day, I went down to Southern Area to see the boys (2/2 G.R.) in their new quarters – about half an hour's walk straight up the main road to Changi village. They are not badly off down there, for space, but they have become rather split up as they're all living in pairs in blocks of small cubicles (once termed 'superior personnel' lines, for Malays!), so they only see as much of each other as they want to, except in the Mess which they are sharing with the 2/9th officers.

The Japs gave us all postcards last week to send off to our folks the same as in June last year, only we were allowed a few more words (up to 24). I only hope and pray they reach their destinations – of course we don't even know if the other cards got home or not.

We have been having some very excellent lectures lately. One on the 'Battle of France' by a fellow who went through it all with the Grenadier Guards; he had previously given a talk on his time with the Guards at home – he was a P.S.M. at the time and had some unique experiences, e.g. being one of the pall-bearers at the funeral of King George V – doing sentry outside Buckingham Palace gates. Then one padre Duckworth, who was cox to the Cambridge boat in 1934, '35, and '36, came over and told us of his experiences – one of the most amusing talks I have ever listened to. A couple of nights ago, Warrington (an officer in this Mess) talked on the Battle of Britain – very enlightening to many of us who had not been at home during the war; he is going to deal with the night-bombing side of it in another talk.

Also had some good entertainment last week. The 18 Div. D.C. put on 'Badger's Green' at the Palladium Theatre in the Hospital area (this is the original Changi Cinema, which is now used for plays and concerts, etc.) – full stage lighting effects and fans working – an excellently produced and acted show but a decidedly weak plot (written by the author of 'Journey's End' and I believe this play only ran for three weeks in London). The next show on there is a promenade concert which I'm very anxious to get down to. On Sunday last we had a visit by the 18 Div. Swing band to the Convalescent Depot in our area. No less than four of the band are professionals – two American and two English, one of the latter having been Jack Hylton's double-bass player – so the result, as you may imagine, is a dance band which would do credit to any London night club.

Did one a lot of good to listen to that sort of thing.

(Many years later he added 'or did it?'!)

Thursday 11 March

The great news of the moment is the arrival of a huge quantity of mail –
something in the neighbourhood of 120,000 letters for the whole camp,
including Indian troops. Certain officers from each unit have been up
sorting them at Jap H.Q. and almost every person one meets has heard
by now that he has got one letter or more to his name; quite a few know
they have at least ten and one lucky individual has been informed that
no less than 26 of his letters have been seen during the sorting. I seem
to have drawn a blank so far but I'm going down to Changi village this
evening to see if any of the 28 Bde. sorters have seen anything (today
being my Thursday holiday). It is not known yet whether the Japanese
are going to censor all the mail; if they do it will take about three months.
The hope is that they will censor just a few and, if they are satisfied with
the general trend of news given, that they will push out the remainder to
us uncensored.

Quite a lot doing during past week: Cricket match on Wednesday
versus the A.O.R.s of the group. Thursday was my holiday – went
visiting various people in Hospital (including 'Uncle' who was in great
form and has since come out) and managed to scrounge some tickets for
the Symphony concert at the Palladium that evening (excellent show –
was given another ticket on Tuesday and went again). Friday, was our
night for the A.I.F. concert – still changing programme every fortnight
and well worth going to.

I had a look, yesterday, at some of the work of the Australian official
War Artist; some of his stuff was excellent, I thought, but did not
appreciate the majority – too surrealistic tendences for my liking.

Col. Hughes, commanding the G.&W. area over the road, came across
to dine with us last night – very nice man – a Mountain Gunner who had
been fairly lately in Razmak and Dehra Dun.

Been having rather a lot of rain lately – always in the evenings, resulting
in two or three of our biweekly unit lectures having to be cancelled. But
did have one interesting talk about ten days ago: this was by a member
of the crew of a British merchant vessel which, on her maiden voyage
from home, had been torpedoed and sunk in the South Atlantic by a fast
German raider. The crew of 28 were brought in here, via Batavia, about
three weeks ago, as well as crew off an American and Greek ship both
sunk by the same raider. This German ship had been away from Germany

about 3 years and had accounted for 14 allied ships. The lecturer was full of praise for the excellent treatment they received on board after capture and had many interesting things to tell us of the outside world (for they were free men only about 11 weeks ago).

There was quite an interesting 'General Order' from the Japanese yesterday to the effect that they are expecting air raids on Singapore Island any time from now on and that if any man should pick up any leaflets or arms which may be dropped, he would be shot.

So, on with the bombs (as long as they don't hit us).

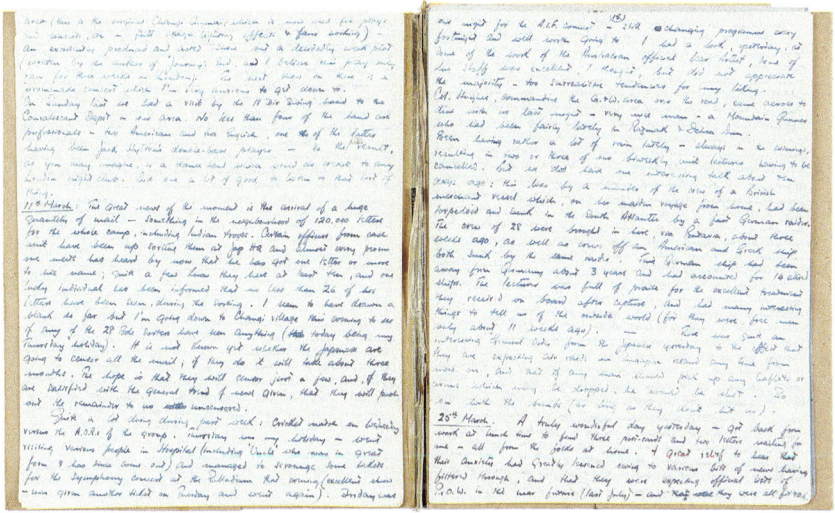

Two pages of the diary, written on exceptionally thin paper

Thursday 25 March – First letters received

A truly wonderful day yesterday – got back from work at lunch time to find three post-cards and two letters waiting for me – all from the folks at home. A great relief to hear that their anxiety had greatly lessened owing to various bits of news having filtered through and that they were expecting official lists of P.O.W.s in the near future (last July) – and that they were all fit and O.K.

I had heard about ten days ago that six letters for me had been seen during the sorting but one of those was from my brother in India which I haven't received yet, so I must have at least one more from home (as I had not been told of the one from my sister which came yesterday).

Alec Ogilvie has also heard from Camberley and Bob Skene from his wife in Australia. The most depressing piece of news is with regard to Geoffrey Woollcombe; up till now we had been setting all our hopes on his having got back to India but the latest bombshell is that a letter has arrived for him from India, addressed as 'last seen leaving Sumatra' etc. so there is presumably very little hope.

Quite a lot doing lately: dinner in the Gurkha Mess last Thursday – a skiing meeting on Friday (short talks on technique and skiing in Japan) – Warrington's second talk on the Battle of Britain on Saturday.

Sunday, church in the evening followed by a unique type of entertainment-cum-lecture entitled 'How the Composer works', with illustrations on the piano – very instructive; the lecturer was in charge of music in Singapore in peace and a very accomplished fellow indeed.

On Tuesday Alec and I were given seats to what I'm sure must be the best musical show which has yet been produced in Changi – 'Dancing Tears' at the Palladium (in the Hospital area) – a musical show portraying nightclubs and cabarets in different parts of the world – excellent production and lighting effects and, of course, the dance band which we heard two or three weeks ago up in this area. Earlier last week, incidentally, we saw the anniversary show of the A.I.F. concert party, containing all the high-lights from their past shows. They've done a wonderful job of work, that crowd.

My patch of garden is progressing well; have just finished planting it up with sweet potatoes, leaving a couple of blocks of beds for experimental purposes, to see what will be most suitable to plant as a second crop.

As a matter of interest I have roughly 40 blocks of beds, with 14 beds to the block and an average of 80 plants to a bed, working out at 44,800 plants (all potatoes)!!

Thursday 8 April

Things are moving fast. We have just this moment heard that there is to be another big move ex. Changi some time during the following week – most or all of the Dutch (about 5,000) and 7,000 British and Australian composed of: 3,000 A.I.F., 15,000 from the G.&W. area over the road and the remainder from Southern Area and 18 Div.

That will probably leave something under 10,000 in the whole camp. The proportion of officers to go is not yet known.

The party are to go (so the Japs say) by rail, to a destination of similar climate to this – and that they will have to build the camp on arrival. I had not mentioned that a party of 5,000 left about a month ago (½ British and ½ Australian) closely followed by another party of 2,000 (forget composition).

This looks very much like the final clear out, as of the 10,000 remaining about 5,000 are either in Hospital, sick or unfit. It remains to be seen how this is going to affect the gardens but it seems pretty safe to say that we (the officers of the Garden Control Group) will not be going. On the other hand it looks very much as if this is where Alec and I do our final split with 2 G.R. and 28 Bde. Anyway – we shall see.

Received a very welcome letter from my brother in India, last week – separate from my other mail. They still seem to be dishing out mail – I am expecting at least one more from home, which I have been told about.

Talking of mail, they are now passing round a home news sheet comprising selected extracts of interesting items of news from home (and India and Australia); most interesting reading – we wonder, how on earth some of the news ever got past the censors (mentions of units by name etc.).

Have played cricket 3 or 4 times during the past 6 weeks or so, with the usual piffling results I invariably do achieve in that game – nevertheless they were amusing afternoons, for the most part.

Sunday 11 April

I have recently finished quite a lengthy session of dentistry; went down with the idea of having my teeth cleaned up and he promptly found 7 fillings. He did some excellent work and I hope I am set up for another six months or so.

Rained hard last Saturday week (all day) so we had a day in; but since then not a drop and a very strong sun all and every day, with the result that the gardens are getting dangerously dry and we are having to hold hard with all planting (I want to put in a block of brinjals – egg fruit – to see how they go).

We have had two large harvestings during the past fortnight – over 5,000 lbs of greenery on each occasion (including about 500 lbs of green potato 'tips' off my patch – 2 or 3 inches off the end of the new shoots).

With the great decrease in numbers here the garden should be of really great value, considering the size it has now grown to.

The latest news with regard to the projected move is that we may have to lose one or two of the Australian Officers from our G.C.G; also the fact that we can pretty safely say that no one from the Second Gurkhas will be going. They may very well be coming back to the Selerang Square barracks again.

John Meillon (our unit Adjutant – an Australian) went into Hospital last Wednesday for another operation on his leg which has been giving him more trouble (a war wound). I took him and one or two others along to the last night of 'Dancing Tears' but they unfortunately fooled the show up to such a degree – being the last night – that it was almost ruined for anyone who had not seen it before; not one single scene was played straight and the band was the only feature that made it enjoyable.

The following morning – Thursday – being my day off – a lot of us forgathered at 11 a.m. at the 'Changi Restaurant', which we had heard a lot about. It's a place run by the Dutch, in 18 Div. area, where they have on sale hot sweet coffee (3c a cup) and all sorts and shapes of small eats – not at all a bad place. We stayed on till about 1.30 p.m., missed lunch and got back here at 3 p.m. feeling very well fed – but having spent a whole dollar – a considerable sum in this place.

Fortunately most of us have got $5.00 extra pay this month, so we almost feel like millionaires.

We still get all the usual things through the Canteens. I find that my main necessities are, first, tobacco – Javanese cigarette tobacco at about 25c per oz. (slightly cheaper if bought in bulk, which I now do), not bad stuff and infinitely preferable to most of the cheap Chinese cigarettes; (I've been rolling my own for the last six months or so now). Then, secondly, Gula Malacca or sweet syrup to put on the breakfast rice porridge, and thirdly peanuts which the mess roasts for us – great vitamin givers and damned good to eat. Apart from these I occasionally stand myself a couple of eggs, when they are in and the occasional bar of carbolic soap and toothpaste etc. And there's really nothing else one wants (much!).

Monday 19 April

A second batch of mail is in and so far I have done wonderfully well six letters and a p.c. – and high hopes of yet more.

The move ex-Changi is in full swing: most of the Dutch went off last week – about five parties of 600 each and now the Australians have started. All parties leave the camp at the un-christian hour of 4.30 a.m. and it appears they will be leaving daily at that hour for the next fortnight or three weeks. The first Aussie party must have had a pretty tough time on Sunday night – there was a tropical downpour of rain lasting the whole night with hardly a five minutes let up.

Much rain by day, too, which is pepping up the garden very well and I was able to get in my block of brinjals.

From today onwards I have taken on an additional area – just opposite my present one and much the same size: about a third of it is already planted out (potatoes), some parts bedded but unplanted and a small area not yet bedded.

The three Australian officers are not going up-country after all, so our Mess will remain the same as before, though we have lost about 80 O.R.s from the G.C.G. We never know, now, from day to day how many we expect out on the gardens; my gang of Manchesters will probably cease coming after Thursday (they are train No. 9). The 18 Div. Dance band were playing every night last week at the Changi Restaurant and we had a very excellent party there on Wednesday night – one somehow acquired almost a party spirit (on semi sweetened black coffee!).

Alec and I went over to dine with the Bn. last night, in Changi village. Dob Skene also came down, he works with the forestry party in the G.&W. area over the road. We went on to the Restaurant after dinner – the place seems to be becoming quite a 'habit' with people these days.

Easter Sunday (25th) April. Another crop of five letters yesterday, bringing my total to twenty - a wonderful business; ~~but~~ Alec Ogilvie and I are running neck & neck, and both of us ~~very unpopular with~~ much envied by those who have only had the meagre one or two. — A few days back the Japs made a sudden call for yet another party of 1600 to leave Changi (presumed overseas). We have consequently had to part with our remaining 45 Australians in the Garden Group (all except a few batmen and sick). We gave them a farewell party last night with the aid of a piano and singing, etc., and they all went off this morning at 10 o'clock. We are just waiting for their convoy to come past on the road any moment now. Two convoys of Dutch have already left this morning. — The labour situation on the gardens is very difficult with the greatly reduced numbers. I saw the last of my excellent gang of Manchesters the day before yesterday — they are off tomorrow. We are doing our best to carry on at present with category 'B' medical men (Aussies) — vitamin deficiency chaps, the majority with eye trouble. We have to work ~~them~~ them very lightly — it remains to be seen how long they last out (just been to the balcony to see the boys pass by — shouts of the good old cry: "You'll never get off the —— island!").

Easter Sunday, 25 April

Another crop of five letters yesterday, bringing my total to twenty, wonderful business; Alec Ogilvie and I are running neck and neck and both of us much envied by those who have only had the meagre one or two.

A few days back the Japs made a sudden call for yet another party of 1,600 to leave Changi (presumed overseas).

We have consequently had to part with our remaining 45 Australians in the Garden Group (all except a few batmen and sick). We gave them a farewell party last night with the aid of a piano and singing etc., and they all went off that morning at 10 o'clock.

We are just waiting for their convoy to come past on the road any moment now. Two convoys of Dutch have already left this morning. The labour situation on the gardens is very difficult with the greatly reduced numbers. I saw the last of my excellent gang of Manchesters the day before yesterday – they are off tomorrow. We are doing our best to carry on at present with category 'B' medical men (Aussies) – vitamin deficiency chaps, the majority with eye trouble. We have to work them very lightly – it remains to be seen how long they last out just been to the balcony to see the boys pass by – shouts of the good old cry: 'You'll never get off the —— island!'

Thursday 29 April

The Emperor of Japan's birthday today so we have been given a day's holiday off the gardens (my own normal Thursday holiday so I haven't gained anything). It's a very welcome break, as we ourselves are putting in an extremely strenuous day's manual labour these days.

During the past 10 days I have been running another area as well as my own (see I mentioned this over the page); I have completed the bedding and am handing the area over to Tom Bunning tomorrow.

I keep on with my original patch and will probably only have about ten men to work it.

I had forgotten to mention having seen the production of 'Who killed the Count?' about ten days ago, at the Palladium. A really gripping thriller, excellently acted and produced. The latest A.I.F. show, which we saw a couple of nights ago, was a bit of a change from their normal variety; it was musical comedy (complete with plot) and I think their best effort up to date.

The great exodus still goes on – we get woken up every night by the lorries going by. They have started to close down Southern Area and 18 Div. and all our fellows moved up from Changi village yesterday: 30 of them are quartered in a bungalow not far from us – must go over and see them this evening.

Thursday 6 May

My normal Thursday holiday; no reason for not taking it, as labour has been slightly on the increase lately – not that it will last very long as yet another party of 3,000 has started to leave (commenced Tuesday and finishes Sunday night) – English, Australian and Dutch. We lost seventeen more Aussy O.R.s from the Garden Group and also, most unfortunately, Ron Wait, our interpreter, who was compelled to go, much against his will. We gave him an excellent farewell dinner the evening before last, with two of the garden Japanese as guests – rather an amusing show; they both speak plausible English and were not as shy as I expected.

This latest party reduces the camp to about 6½ thousand. Rumours are rife as to possible future parties (including a large officers' party) and one story is that the whole of Changi will be evacuated by the end of May (!) – but still, nothing definite has come through as yet.

THE TEMPLE PLAYERS

Arms
and the man
by
G·B·Shaw

with

R·H·PANTLING   PETER DICKSON

ALEC OGILVIE   W·HOGG FERGUSON

LESLIE ROGERS   LESLIE OWEN

LESLIE WEST   HARRY GREER

PRODUCED BY   R·H·PANTLING

CHANGI P·O·W·CAMP·MAY 1942

My birthday yesterday, incidentally, as well as that of Mike Cooper who presented me with an excellent cigarette lighter (locally made by a Dutchman). I went down to see him last night in Hospital – he's in with dry pleurisy. My other birthday gift was one small (very small) hen's egg!

We have regular cropping days on the gardens nowadays; I got over a ton of leaf off my patch last time (picked by 10 chaps off only about 8 blocks of beds).

I recently put in a block of amaranth seedlings (spinach family with red leaf) which are doing quite well.

May 6th. My normal Thursday holiday; no reason for not taking it, as labour has been slightly on the increase lately – not that it will last very long as yet another party of 3000 has started to leave (commenced Tuesday & finishes Sunday night) – English, Australian and Dutch. We lost seventeen more Aussy O.R.s from the Garden Group, and also, most unfortunately, Ron Wait our interpreter, who was compelled to go, much against his will. We gave him an excellent farewell dinner the evening before last, with two of the garden Japanese as guests – rather an amusing show; they both speak plausible English and were not as shy as I expected. This latest party reduces the camp to about 6½ thousand. Rumours are rife as to possible future parties (including a large officers' party) and one story is that the whole of Changi will be evacuated by the end of May(!) – but still, nothing definite has come through as yet. – My birthday yesterday, incidentally, as well as that of Mike Cooper who presented me with an excellent cigarette lighter (locally made by a Dutchman). I went down to see him last night in Hospital – he's in with dry pleurisy. My other birthday gift was one small (very small) hen's egg! – We have regular cropping days on the gardens nowadays; I got over a ton of leaf off my patch last time (picked by 10 chaps off only about 8 blocks of beds). I recently put in a block of amaranth seedlings (spinach family with red leaf) which are doing quite well.

Thursday 13 May

As was expected, an all-officers party was detailed a few days back (strength 320), including the majority of the 2nd Gurkha Officers. Alec and I and Bob Skene and others, went over to their farewell dinner party last night.

But – I was on my way over just now to see if I could get on to the loading party down at the station (they were all due to go tonight) and I hear that the whole party is postponed – date of departure unknown. Not really surprising, in view of similar previous episodes. The only officer due to have gone from our group is George Yule, our Q.M.

But there is yet another party of 900 due to leave and on that we are losing about 40 O.R.s, leaving us about 50 strong, including officers. When and if these two parties go, there will be a total of about 5,000 left, of which roughly 3,000 are in Hospital and 800 or so are not fit for fatigues, so we are naturally not expecting many down on the gardens from now on. I have got hold of an excellent iron spring bed, from a fellow gone up country but unfortunately no mattress.

Monday 17 May

Steady rain all the morning so no gardening today. Yesterday the Officers' party were warned that they would be off today, so Alec and I went round after dinner for another evening of farewells. And an excellent party it was: someone produced a couple of bottles of locally brewed 'samshu' – quite potent and we were all in remarkably good form. We didn't get back till 1 a.m., feeling quite definitely 'merry'.

Spent the whole morning, up till lunch, on the square, seeing them all off – 28 to a lorry as well as their portable kit. 'J' Force (the 900) also went off. They had extremely short notice; the message came in about 11.30 on Friday night that they were to move the following morning. They went by sea, as anticipated and we could see what was probably their convoy steaming out yesterday.

I achieved my long awaited trip into Singapore on Friday, when the Jap Sergeant, Iokawa, took some of us in with him in the truck. Raffles Place and the water front etc. was quite interesting, not having been in before. It felt extremely odd being in the middle of a city again, not to mention getting an occasional glimpse of a white (or nearly white) girl for the first time since December 1941! (nearly leaped out of the truck).

Thursday 3 June

A real scorcher of a day on the garden and feeling too exhausted to go out anywhere tonight, so I may as well get this up to date.

Most of us have lately dropped having our usual one day off a week, owing to lack of numbers but think we'll have to start again with weather like this (very dry and hot).

The greatest innovation in the Camp of late has been the starting up of a large restaurant in the old peace-time N.A.A.F.I. building, just off Selarang Square – run on much the same lines as the old Changi village restaurant which we used to visit but a very much bigger show, with a 'floor show' on most nights and catering for at least 300 people.

It's mainly for the benefit of the troops, and officers have a side verandah to themselves with an 'officers only' serving hatch! The coffee and eats are excellent but it is already quite obvious that one can't make a habit of the place as it would very quickly run away with one's entire pay.

Incidentally officers' pay has just been increased, slightly. I now get $22 per month of which $8.80 goes into the Mess.

Another centre of life in the evenings is the Australian Officers' Club. We all went along to its official opening night last week, when Jack Greenwood's band provided an excellent evening's entertainment. There is the usual sweet coffee and small eats to be obtained; but definitely more 'select' than the noise and crowd at 'Smoky Joe's' (above).

The Camp seems to have settled down quite well with the comparatively small numbers now remaining. No rumours of any further moves and it very much looks as if we have seen the last of them.

Golf has been the great programme for a few of us lately, every Wednesday and Sunday afternoon. We have had a bag of clubs with us now for 2 or 3 months but have only recently acquired any balls. Three or four of us go out on the G.&W. area padang, with about 14 balls (in every imaginable stage of shape and decomposition!) and slash back and forth.

We have two scratch golfers in the Mess and I'm all set to come out of here in a similar state.

Tuesday 15 June

I am having rather a welcome respite from the gardens all this week: the M.O. who has been staying with us for the past fortnight has pronounced that I have got Singapore feet – a very common complaint (skin rot between the toes and on the ball of the foot) – and that they will have no chance of healing whilst my feet are in boots all day long. So I am giving them a daily bathe in Condy's Fluid and leading an extremely idle life.

I'm all in favour of it as there's nothing important due to happen on my garden for another three weeks or so when I start to dig up my spuds.

Nothing out of the usual been happening. An amusing golfing afternoon on Sunday when I started off chronically badly but got put back onto the rails again by an Aussy professional who was out for a spot of practice. Went out to dinner last Sunday week with Alex Masters over at the Gurkha Mess and went on to the club where Jack Greenwood was again performing.

They have booked his band now for every other Sunday night and the A.I.F. concert band on every other (alternate) Saturday is a big "do' there every weekend. Saw another Palladium show the other day and the first night of the latest A.I.F. show last night (vastly improved from the usual).

Sunday 27 June

As intended, I stayed off the gardens the whole of last week; it rained all the following Monday so I got that day off as well. Feet perfectly O.K. again. We've had intermittent slight rain during the week and this morning we woke up to real heavy stuff, which I hope will make up for the very dry state the gardens are in. I have been attending one or two interesting meetings during the last two weeks. We have started off our small skiing and mountaineering club again, meeting every Wednesday evening; quite a good programme of interesting talks have been fixed, the first of which we had last Wednesday (skiing reminiscences in various Swiss and Austrian centres).

We are alternating each week between skiing and pure mountaineering (rope dangling, etc). We are only quite a small gathering of about 20 but it is remarkable to find out to what varied places they have been to in this world. I know some may think our Club rather fantastic but it is undoubtedly a great mental stimulant in this hole to sit down and talk snow and mountain memories for a couple of hours or so.

Glan Williams, who used to give those piano lecture-cum-entertainments a few weeks ago, has started up another choir (he ran one last year in Southern Area). We had our first session last Monday evening and will with luck get together every Monday. It is a most entertaining business and reminds me of my school choir days. I was selected as a first tenor – a bit of a strain at first but will probably get used to it.

Every Tuesday evening, nowadays, attend a small photographic club (again, of course all talk – no cameras! – but nevertheless interesting); I managed to get a loan of that excellent volume, the Leica Manual, last week.

A small medical party of 50 M.O.s and 250 med. orderlies left Changi for up-country a couple of days ago. The story is that they are going to be split up among all the other P.O.W. camps (presumably in Malaya and Bangkok etc.). Have managed to get hold of an old British Ski Year Book (1936) so I must away to it.

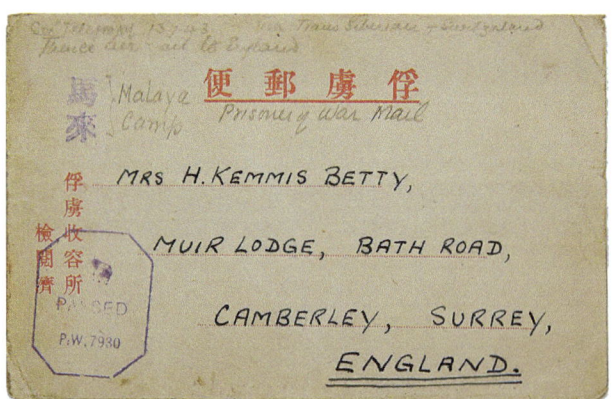

Sunday 1 August

Can think of no reasonable excuse to offer for this rather long lapse, presumably the dullness of life has failed to inspire me to commit anything to paper. Extremely dry weather has been continuing now for well over 2½ months except for intermittent short storms with little or no rain – soil consequently in very powdery state and watering is the chief work on the garden.

Commenced digging up my spuds on about the sixth of the month (July) and have finished just half my area; replanting with red amaranth (spinach) and sword beans, the former requiring much water in their first few days. Very difficult to plant fast enough owing to scorching hot sun and necessity of careful shading with coconut palm fronds.

Today been fairly overcast and a little rain, and weather looks as if it may be on the change. Have ceased taking my Thursday holiday and now take Sunday morning instead – have taken the last four Sundays running and normally go over to a coffee and cake party at the Gurkha Mess (generally quite a large gathering).

Have overspent my pay this month – as usual – and now hear that we are not being paid till the 5th of the month so am experiencing acute shortage of smokes (will have to cut down on visits to Smoky Joe's this month). Our small Alpine club has been proving quite successful – I even rose to give a talk myself last week, on skiing in Kashmir, which seemed to be quite well received. Our Monday evening choral practise is not such a promising business; Glan Williams, our original choir master, is still in hospital and his successor frankly gets on my nerves – much too dramatic and never teaches us anything new.

Renewed talk of moves going round the camp. Seems very possible that the entire Hospital will have to move up into the G.&W. area, over the road. Most unfortunate for them if it materialises as there are no suitable buildings whatsoever over there – only wooden huts – and also the area is still in a filthy state, having had about 2,000 Chinese, Malays and Tamils in there for 3 or 4 days last week (they were being collected by the Japanese for being sent upcountry on some work). Also talk of the entire camp moving

1. to Singapore
2. to Johore Bahru, across the causeway, or
3. to Taiwan(!?)

Sunday 22 August

Another chapter in our Changi existence now commences: the long expected Hospital move (to Selarang Square) is now in operation, thus involving a complete housing reshuffle throughout the whole camp – and our own move last Tuesday over the road to the 'Piggery' area. Not quite as bad as it may sound: the pigs and their whole organisation are quite separate from us. We occupy the cricket pavilion (which used to be the Gurkha Mess) and an attap hut just near to it (in which I live, with eight other officers: Alec and I share a cubicle). We use the pavilion verandah as a Mess and have quite a good little spot for sitting out in the evenings, under a couple of West Indian Cherry Trees, with a view across the G.&W. padang, which we are right next door to but may not use.

There is unfortunately no hutted accommodation for the O.R.s so they are all in tents, pitched around our hut and the pavilion. All rather tight but we shall very soon settle down.

We were lucky to have hung on to our other abode for so long (over nine months – a very long stay in one house for Changi!). Slap opposite my hut is Macgregor's chicken and duck farm – about 250 birds all – not twenty yards away; I expect we shall have to get used to that, as well! The Hospital move is to be completed by next Saturday and then the whole camp, except ourselves and Piggery, will be in the old A.I.F. area.

As can be imagined the move is taking many men away from the gardens; yesterday I only had 5 men on my area – very difficult to carry on with so few but it will only be for a week. The long drought, of over 2 months, has at last broken; the weather has completely changed and we are getting rain almost every other day now and the gardens have perked up wonderfully. This is my usual Sunday holiday (yesterday afternoon as well) which I intend sticking to.

Nearly forgot to mention that during the past ten days or so, the second batch of mail has been trickling slowly out from the gaol (limited number being censored every day); have already clocked in seven, both from home and India and was much elated, but I can see there are a good few missing and am hoping any day for a large haul. (Alec O. got ten in one evening!) All the home letters are dated about Sept. or Oct. 1942 – nearly a year old – but they are truly wonderful to get, however old.

There have been two interesting lectures lately by fellows captured by the Japs in Burma and brought in here about a month ago. Both of them members of Wingate's guerrillas, and we learn that our 3rd Bn. was one of the three Bns.

Other chaps who were brought in were two American airmen – the young pilot and co-pilot of a Liberator brought down near Mergui – they also have a very thrilling story to relate. Also another guerrilla bloke who was at Sandhurst with me and knew many of my Bradfield contemporaries. Have had two evenings of tennis during the past fortnight, down on a court which they had got going in the Hospital area. This move puts an end to that court but we think we can renovate an old court below Smoky Joe's.

I hope so, as there are quite a few keen players who have collected passable rackets from God knows where and we even possess 5 brand new balls.

Sunday 5 September

Nothing worth writing about. Four years of war gone by – four too many. My last sheet of this airmail paper, having used the rest as cigarette paper. I am seriously considering smoking the whole diary!

A batch of 200,000 more letters are reported to have arrived, so let's hope they are of later vintage than the others.

The Australian officers' club has temporarily closed down and Smoky Joe's has not reopened since the move, so we now have nowhere to go coffee-housing in the evenings – possibly a good thing as we'll save a bit of money.

A pleasant evening on Friday when John S. came round and read extracts of his book and short stories; we had a small 'cook-up' – potato and onion rissoles fried in coconut oil and sweet coffee with coconut milk (a really excellent drink).

Scott and I went round to his Mess last night to see a cinema show – very ancient Harold Lloyds, Charlie Chaplins and Popeye the Sailors, etc. – quite amusing.

The C.O. and Bob Skene are dining over here this evening, followed by bridge with Alec and Duke Warrington, while I go to church and return in time to join them at further coffee and rissoles – and such is life.

Wednesday 22 September

Another letter from home this evening, making seven or eight in this batch and a total of 34. No confirmed news of me, unfortunately, when the latest letters were written (January 1943). Hope to God they have heard by now. The autumn wet season appears to have commenced – we have had four or five days off for rain during the past fortnight. The weather is gradually swinging round to the north for the N.E. monsoon. The main business affecting life at present is a large daily working party of 900 which the Japanese are employing in the construction of a new air landing ground.

We evidently put up an official strong complaint against doing such work for them but they countered that by saying that it was playing fields which were under construction and not an air strip (the place is about 300yds by 1,500yds).

They are employing local Asiatics as well as a few Indian troops for the job; we pass them all coming through on lorries on our way down to the gardens in the morning. Our chaps all march down (the ground is in the old Southern Area and Hospital areas) about 9am and get back about 6pm – a long day and many of them are far from being category 'A' fit.

The result is, naturally, that our gardens are suffering heavily from the labour point of view. I think the final decision (by the Japs) is that we get a maximum of 200 as long as the air strip fatigue is in progress, which may be a good few months. Just completed, this morning, digging up all my spuds. Busy now in re-bedding and planting with amaranth and more spuds.

Another Java party – 500 strong – passed through the camp last week – the first batch, so they say, of about 3,000 still due to come over from Java. Only about 150 of them were Dutch, the remainder British R.A.F., R.A., Australians and Americans. I had some of them on my garden just for one morning. Had another attempt at tennis this evening, foiled by rain. They've got a court going, now, just off Selarang Square.

I was lucky to get 40 sheets of this paper, 20 for diary and 20 I have set aside for cigarette paper (a bit thick but infinitely better than newspaper).

Our mountain club has been keeping us amused on Wednesday nights. A talk two weeks back on skiing in Australia decreased my desire to visit Mt. Kosiosko – evidently no runs anywhere exceeding 2,000 feet and weather generally uncertain. 'Bonzo' Moore tonight on skiing technique (which should lead to heated arguments on balance and swing etc), and next week Scott on his Karakoram expedition.

Sunday 25 September

Very relieving piece of news last night, in my latest letter from home (dated and Feb. '43); they had just had the official India Office telegram to the effect that I was a P.O.W. – so I'm hoping that may have eased the anxiety a great deal.

It's a wonderful thing this mail, which I have been getting in ones and twos every two or three days for the past fortnight. And the sorters say that it is by no means finished yet.

Having another attempt at tennis this evening – hope the weather holds – it is very uncertain nowadays.

Sunday 3 October

Tennis last Sunday and Wednesday was a great success – felt almost at home at it. Will have to give it a miss today owing to a huge blister in the palm of my hand from planting sweet potatoes with a 'dibble stick' (shockingly thin nib this pen has got – my own I am hoping to sell for a few dollars as we are expecting our pay to go down with a bump this month). Just trying another – with crossed nib!

Went out to dinner with John Stephens last Wednesday and brought back his book entitled 'Gurkha Retrospect' – his own experiences in India from the time he joined his Regt. up till leaving Razmak in 1941 – a very creditable effort. He's written quite a lot of other stuff during our sojourn here.

Another Java party of 2,500 arrived a couple of days ago; about a thousand of them are due to remain while the remainder will go on shortly, to a further destination. We had 200 of them out gardening yesterday (in addition to our usual lot) of which 15 were on my patch. It is very interesting to meet all these chaps from Java. The officer on my area was Royal Canadian Air Force and most of the Other Ranks R.A.F. In some ways they were extremely well off in Java (eggs 4 cents, as opposed to 28c in our canteens here; sugar 16c a kilo – 75c a lb. here! etc., etc.) – but they seemed very glad to be in an English camp and were very enthusiastic about getting out on the gardens. We hope to get them down as a permanent party.

Been having a few 'black out' and 'brown out' schemes lately, in conjunction with similar shows going on in Singapore; two sirens in the camp wailing all the evening – orders for no smoking outside – no noise etc. All rather annoying but we wouldn't really object to seeing a few allied planes over here!

We hope to throw quite a major party next Sunday night, to mark the anniversary of the formation of the Garden Group (which it will be, to the day; Alec and I joined early in November, a few weeks after it had got going). We are getting over the Jack Greenwood band and various entertainers from the A.I.F. concert party and throwing round a bit of food and drink – should be quite a good show – as parties go in this place.

Monday 11 October

Our party last night was a magnificent success. We had quite a hectic day getting the Supply Depot hall ready – decorations, stage and seating etc.: my little flower garden round the hut on my area came in very useful. Bob S., our interpreter, is no mean artist and did some excellent little water colour sketches for the programmes and large murals, portraying certain characters and typical gardening incidents. We had all the cream of Changi artists, the highlight of the evening being the drummer in Porter's Band – none other than Jack Payne's drummer, recently arrived in the last Java party – a real top notcher in his line and truly remarkable to see in action. The C.O. came over from the hospital where he is getting over a spot of his old trouble. We laid on some very good 'eats' and sweet coffee in the interval (excellent rissoles flavoured with artichokes off Duke's area).

We had to keep strictly to the timed programme, the party finishing at 10 p.m., as we all have to get back over the road by 10.20. (We have recently had considerable trouble from the Jap sentries, one of whom is apt frequently to be difficult. He chased me off the road the other night at the point of the bayonet for no apparent reason.)

Alec is taking part in the production of 'Outward Bound', just commenced at the new Palladium theatre (old Smoky Joe's building) and owing to all this trouble and difficulty about our visiting the main camp area after roll call, he is living over at the Forestry mess until the conclusion of his play (another three weeks or so). So I'm alone in my room.

As we go out so little in the evenings now, a few of us (Scott, Duke etc.) occasionally while away the dark hours with a private 'cook-up' (!)

– usually sweet potato and onion rissoles fried in coconut oil, plus sweet coffee with 'Santan'. This latter is made by first grinding the coconut into fine shreds then squeezing the semi oily juice out through a piece of strong linen (in actual fact a pair of Duke's shorts made from a tent is at present doing the job admirably); this juice strongly resembles very creamy milk with a coconuty flavour and, with a little sugar purchased from the canteen, makes really beautiful coffee. People in this country evidently used santan in their coffee even in normal peacetime.

I feel it would highly amuse anyone from the outside world to see us sitting down for a solid hour or more, clad in towels, pouring with sweat from the exertion of squeezing out enough milk for one cup of coffee per head!

Officers' pay was reduced this month from $22 to $12, so we in this unit have abolished separate officers' Mess and we all feed from the mens' cookhouse, paying only $3 each mess sub. The food has been excellent – just as good as before when we paid in 9 dollars (!), except that we get slightly fewer fried things (coconut oil costing 70c a pint). We are left with just about enough cash for smokes and a little extra fried bread for breakfast (I have gone off rice porridge – gula malacca too expensive).

Had received no mail during the past fortnight and was beginning to think I had got my quota but got another three from home last night – all fairly old, filling up a few gaps in the family story. Still getting Java party chaps down on the gardens but different men each day   Dutch yesterday and today. We lay on an excellent stew in the afternoon break period (3–3.20) – 'jungle stew' as we call it, consisting of everything we can get off the garden, all thrown into the same pot, with a spot of salt.

Each area runs its own show. A great thing for the men, some of whom still get very poor lunches sent down from camp. We also have quite an assortment of wild fruit growing down there. The guava season has just finished and the rambutans should soon be coming along (small prickly skinned fruit very similar to the 'lichee' we get in India). They are followed by the Cachou nut which has a very juicy little pear-shaped fruit growing on the end of the nut. Other fruits are durians, jackfruit, blimbings, mangosteens and chicons – and others! All excellent in their own peculiar way.

The importance of the garden working parties

Details from the Ford Museum, Singapore

1. Tapioca, sweet potato and yam were widely cultivated as they could grow in poor soil conditions and required little care. These hardy crops were the main substitutes for rice which was in very short supply. Peter mentions that they came to the end of a week where in his vegetable gardens they had successfully planted close to 45,000 sweet potato plants. The sweet potato and yam were high in fibre and rich in vitamin C and B6 as well as minerals such as manganese and potassium.

2. Finely cut tapioca skin was used like mee sua (thin noodles) and powdered tapioca was used as flour to make biscuits, snacks and cakes.

3. POWs made a tobacco substitute by mixing yellow papaya leaves with Gula Melaka (palm sugar) and drying the mixture under the sun before chopping it up.

4. Due to the shortage of sugar some people turned to producing their own substitute sweetness by boiling sugar cane juice to make molasses.

5. In Changi, because palm oil was rich in vitamin A, it was treated as equivalent of cod liver oil. Palm oil was used when other cooking oils such as groundnut oil ran short and it was also used as a substitute for ghee.

6. Papaya fruit was not only sweet but high in vitamin A and C and folate.

7. Com and raji (finger fillet) were eaten to prevent beri beri, a disease caused by vitamin B1 deficiency. Raji was cooked like sago and eaten with scraped coconut. Raji was also mixed with corn and tapioca flour to make bread and chapati when wheat flour was unavailable. (Some prisoners remember the results to be rubbery or so hard that "it could be used to kill a man with a loaf of bread".)

8. Lalang is a type of grass native to S.E. Asia and believed to contain medicinal properties by traditional Chinese medical practitioners. It was used as a medicinal herb and POWs drank lalang juice to help combat malnutrition.

Friday 26 November

A cold rainy morning and the day has just been declared a holiday, so here's a chance of breaking my long spell of idleness.

Alec returned about a fortnight ago (from living over the other side); his play 'Outward Bound' was really excellent – quite the best show Changi has seen for many a month. They are putting on 'Hay Fever' in January.

This gardening business seems to be almost my whole life these days. The Java party eventually all departed, so for the past three weeks or so we have been reduced to our normal small numbers. But some of the British upcountry parties are expected to return in the very near future and they'll probably be called upon to swell the garden numbers. We don't quite know which parties are returning but they are expected to include the officers' party on which Uncle Evans and the rest went. It would be good to see them again.

To accommodate them all, wooden (attap) huts have been hastily erected on the old G.&W. padang – just opposite us, so our days of quiet seclusion may be at an end.

The rainy season is well set in now – almost too much rain – the lack of sun is slowing up growth. We get an average of at least one day a week off for rain and frequently get driven home by sudden storms; but as long as there's a good book I don't object. Just finished 'Berlin Diary' (Shiver, American news correspondent), excellent reading – and now on to Lockhart's 'Memoirs of a British Agent'. For the past month or more now I have been regularly attending German classes again (a very good instructor in the X-ray dept. of the hospital) – and I come back a little early on Tuesdays and Fridays for the class from 5 to 6.

Our choir under Glan Williams is going really strong these days – two practices a week – Monday and Friday. The Mountain club is still producing some good lectures: an excellent talk two evenings ago on ski-touring in Spring in the Mont Blanc district.

Thoughts turning once again to Christmas. No Red X ship in this time, I fear, but we have a little poultry up our sleeve, all ready for the pot, and the piggery will probably do some slaughtering. They killed off 14 pigs about a fortnight ago which just gave every man in the camp an ounce or two – the first meat we had tasted for many a month. There was also a small Jap pork issue last week – I hope they continue it.

Some of us invested in a few 3-day-old ducklings the other day (57 cents each) which should be producing eggs about 6 months hence! They are very frail little beggars during their first 2 or 3 weeks and are quite apt to die off, especially in this rainy weather; but they are now in the capable, loving hands of old broody hen and so far there have been no deaths in the family.

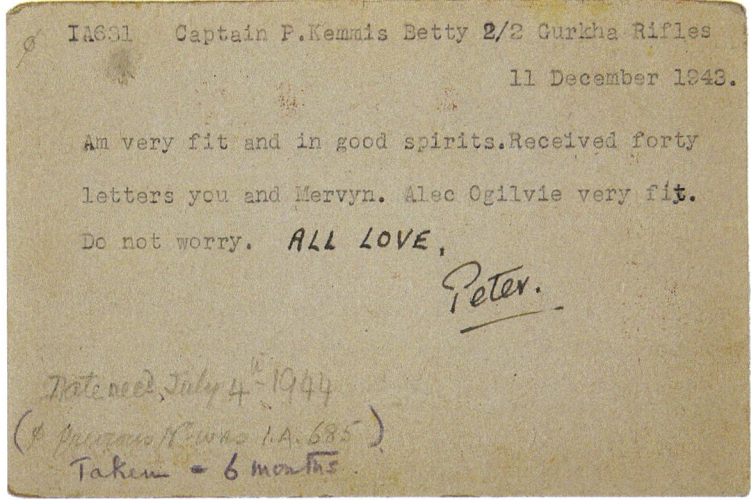

IA831   Captain P.Kemmis Betty 2/2 Gurkha Rifles

11 December 1943.

Am very fit and in good spirits.Received forty

letters you and Mervyn. Alec Ogilvie very fit.

Do not worry. *ALL LOVE,*

Peter.

Date recd. July 4ᵗʰ 1944

(Previous Cards IA.685)

Taken = 6 months .

Card sent on 11 December 1943, arrived 4 July 1944

Saturday 18 December

An appalling story of horror comes from upcountry. I shall go into no detail here – enough to say that in the making of the Jap railway into Burma over 50,000 lives were lost, of which about 40,000 were natives and 10,000 allied P.O.W.s (English, Australian and Dutch) – from this camp. Causes: cholera, dysentery, malaria, tropical ulcers, etc., etc., etc ... The highest death rate was amongst the English.

Only a party of 500 Australians arrived so far and we're urgently awaiting news of the English parties. A truly dreadful thing to come at Christmas time – and much depression throughout the camp.

We were all allowed to send off another 24 word postcard on the 11th of the month (I doubt if it will reach home before we do) and we have now just been granted a very limited number of wireless messages, which is much more to the point – if they ever go. Ronald Coleman won the draw for the officers of our group and he is including all our names and units in his message.

A surprising arrival from Canada the other day – a letter from Winnie Caldwell dated Aug. 27th 1943; it came over on the same ship which brought mail for the Americans here. Great to get news less than four months old: all well in the family but poor old Uncle Don and Doris both dead (cannot understand the latter). She also says re Mervyn – 'a chance he may return' – sounds very odd; M. going back to England??

Have taken today off instead of tomorrow (Sunday), as Duke W. and I have laid on a stupendous lunch, at the expense of a huge drake he has been fattening for the past two months. Which reminds me – our eight little ducklings are going along extremely well; we have recently made an addition to the family of one ¾ grown duck and two younger ducklings. The former is expected to start laying in a month or so.

Have been carrying out some sweeping changes in my garden lately: planted nearly an acre of tapioca in a bad patch of rather sour soil where nothing else did very well. Most of us have come to prefer tapioca to sweet potatoes nowadays (the root is boiled in the same way). Must now go and help with the preparing of this great meal.

Later ... it was Terrific!

A drawing of the gardens, attached to the Christmas lunch menu

1944

Saturday 1 January

> 1st. Jan. 1944 : Well, all our Christmasing and New-Year's-Eveing is behind us and we shall soon be settling down to normal routine again. It all went off very well, considering; plenty of good food & entertainment. Went to some recordings of Handel's "Messiah" at 11 p.m. on Christmas Eve, followed by Holy Communion. Got a late extension that night till 1 a.m. Christmas Day we most of us spent visiting our friends over the road; excellent food all day, although, apart from a pork issue from the Piggery, nothing much out of the ordinary. We were to have eaten some cockerels & ducks but finally decided to present them to the hospital where we hear they provided invaluable chicken broth for about 30 of the worst patients from up-country (not capable of eating solids).

Well, all our Christmasing and New Year's Eve-ing is behind us and we shall soon be settling down to normal routine again.

It all went off very well, considering; plenty of good food and entertainment. Went to some recordings of Handel's 'Messiah' at 1 p.m. on Christmas Eve, followed by Holy Communion.

Got a late extension that night till 1 a.m. Christmas Day we most of us spent visiting our friends over the road; excellent food all day, although, apart from a pork issue from the Piggery, nothing much out of the ordinary. We were to have eaten some cockerels and ducks but finally decided to present them to the hospital where we hear they provided invaluable chicken broth for about 30 of the worst patients from up-country (not capable of eating solids).

On Christmas Night there was most unfortunately a practice blackout (of which we have had many during the past few weeks) which put a stop to a small piano and sing-song entertainment we had laid on. Last night they gave us another extension of lights-out till 1 a.m. A few of us went to the A.I.F. theatre to see the first night of their pantomime – 'Dick Whittington' – a brilliant effort – then back to our rooms for some eats and sweet coffee where we 'saw-the-New-Year-in'.

Scotty had also rigged up our piano just outside our Mess, on the edge of the padang, for the benefit of all, including some of the upcountry men billeted in the new huts – they were most appreciative (Glan Williams at the piano).

A holiday for all today and I think I shall make a proper weekend out of it by taking tomorrow morning off – Sunday – as well.

Much talk of a Red X ship having docked but so far no visible evidence (the hospital are shouting for medical equipment especially with all the new upcountry patients – and we wouldn't mind tasting bully beef again.)

We have had the very welcome news that all the 2/2 G. officers who went upcountry have come through alive (although many had ulcers, etc.) and are in a camp in Singapore; nothing known as to whether they will stay in there or not. Just finished that excellent book of Douglas Reed's 'A Prophet at Home' – I had never read his others.

Early 1944

US submarines enjoyed success destroying
Japanese shipping, especially oil tankers.

25 February

A long lapse since last writing. Life is much the same as ever. A spot of mail came in early in the month – 8 from Mervyn but only one from home. We were expecting very much more. The garden is recovering from a longish spell of dry weather (no rain at all from 10th Jan to 9th Feb) and the last 24 hours have been rather too wet – parts of the lower areas completely under water.

Alec's show 'Hay Fever' has been the outstanding entertainment since the New Year – very excellent – have seen it twice; it still has another week to run, which will total 5½. He'll be returning 'home' next week.

A pleasant Sunday afternoon outing of late has been a bathing party, down in the sea just near by; only about 20 minutes walk and excellent value if the tide is at all high. The first time we went we struck a flat low tide and had to wade out about 300 yds before we reached water deep enough to swim properly.

We unfortunately had to part with John Meillon the other day; he was ordered off to do some Staff Captain job with the A.I.F. units in G.&W. area. He has been replaced by Austen Edwards.

Have been learning Spanish during the past six weeks! Thought that a little more mental exercise wouldn't do me any harm – and it seems a very easy and attractive lingo.

Food has been decidedly on the down-grade lately. Canteen prices are rising to ridiculous heights and very little cooking oil can be obtained (coconut or palm). Eggs we never see – they long ago rose to over 60c. each! We have practically nothing to spend our money on except smokes (the Officers Club had to close down) – and even smokes are getting scarce; the last lot of cheroots and cigarettes had to be rationed throughout the camp so that everyone should get a few. It wouldn't surprise me if they cease to come in altogether. The stew which we have on the gardens everyday counts for a lot with the result that gardening is the most popular fatigue in the camp nowadays.

Our choir has just started to make its presence felt. For the past three weeks we have put on small performances on Sunday nights in the Hospital wards and last night we gave our first real 'public performance' over in the little G.&W. area theatre. We had the camp's two crack soloists – violin and piano – to fill in the gaps between our bursts of song and I think the show went over very well. We repeat the same programme tonight and tomorrow night in the Command Theatre.

Sunday 26 March

Have just completed a most excellent week's holiday over in the 'Gurkha Mess' (with Derek Robertson, John Stephens, Mike Cooper and all the others). I had been pondering the idea for quite a time and took my opportunity when the weather was particularly dry and the garden was indeed becoming rather exhausting.

I had no idea that one could get such a complete change within the confines of Changi. The Mess is probably the best situated building in the camp and, as possibly mentioned before, has a superb view north over the Johore Straits and to the hills beyond. I have been spending my time in exactly the manner I intended, namely being completely idle, reading and sitting out on the lawn, etc.

The first three nights were taken up with our choral concert which we gave at the A.I.F. theatre – an hour and a half programme, with solo flute, piano and vocal performers to fill the gaps between our choir items. By all reports the show seems to have gone down well. On the Thursday night we all had invitations to a classical concert in the Hospital Theatre.

Our choir (or the 'Glee Singers' as we call ourselves) have been lucky enough to be included in the programmes of broadcasts which have been recently made from the camp.

This morning we forgathered at the Hospital Theatre for a rehearsal; quite an entertaining morning. Four complete 15-20 min. programmes were rehearsed, in one of which we put over two numbers (only 5 minutes singing). The great thing is that we all get our names over the air (if the Japs ever do broadcast them). We expect the actual recordings to be made any time in the near future – no date yet given.

We were warned the other day for an inspection of Changi by a Jap Staff officer of the P.O.W. Information Bureau. It was to have taken place on Sat., was then put off till today and is now further postponed. That is why I delayed my departure back 'home'. I shall definitely return tomorrow morning after breakfast; hope there has been some activity on my area during my absence.

Support from the Church and Clergy

Outside Changi, on the island of Singapore, a Federation of Christian Churches was organised and this had the support of the Japanese.

Inside Changi makeshift sheds were built to serve chapels, seven in total, in the Changi Village area. The weekly services were packed. There was a service every Sunday and often there were midweek services as well. Blackcurrant jam was boiled up and bottled as communion wine and the unleavened bread made from rice flour, maize and tapioca.

There were as many as 30 clergy or chaplins in Changi who worked tirelessly to minister to the spiritual needs of every denomination. A special mention is given to Bishop Wilson for his extraordinary strength in adversity and his religious leadership helping to maintain the morale of the prisoners, sometimes at great cost to his own health and safety.

Revd Lewis Bryan, who was also an internee at Changi, wrote: 'Many officers and men openly stated that it was their religion – the sacraments and services of their churches – which kept them sane, when everything men hold dear was lost.'

Good Friday, 7 April

My chaps got through a wonderful amount of planting during my week away from the garden. Been very hot and dry during the past fortnight but the weather looks as if it's on the change (a small shower this morning).

Today, being my usual Friday off, Duke and I went down and had a swim with the No. 2 area party (who go down daily). Tide was right up and extremely pleasant but we arrived back with rather too much of an appetite for lunch, which was pitifully small. The food situation has deteriorated considerably lately; only about 8oz. rice per man per day, 'black' beans cut down and very little vegetable coming in. Fortunately we are still getting small issues of meat about three times a week which saves the situation. But still, I expect we shall have to be prepared for things to get steadily worse. The canteen prices are also becoming farcical; sugar 3.20 per lb., Gula Malacca $2.75, peanuts over 3.00! And the normal sized cheroot which at one time cost 2 or 3 cents each have risen to 8 and 10 cents – and daily increasing in price. Our daily garden stew means more and more to us these days and the disadvantage of a day off is that one gets so damned hungry!

I had forgotten to mention that a small consignment of Red X food arrived about six weeks ago – intended for the Americans in the camp but as there were only about 30 of them it was divided round the whole camp – very small amounts – and we spun it out over a month. It included 28 Camels or Chesterfields each which 'sucked down' very well. Had quite a shock when I weighed myself the other day and only clocked exactly 10 stone and then with shorts, shoes and socks on.

The camp is once more in the throws of hectic internal moves owing, mainly, to the Japs having ordered that no tents may any longer be occupied – also they have taken over five or six houses, thus shoving the camp up tighter. We are so far unaffected except that we may get one extra officer to live with us.

To-night Van and I are singing in a special little Good Friday service at which a type of 'Curtain' Passion Play is being put on – we form part of an octet who every now and then chip in with hymns, psalms and anthems etc.

Easter Monday is a holiday for all and Alec and I intend to devour our two drakes, which were left over from the eight or nine we had to get rid of – with the six other O.R.s we get ¼ bird each!

Wednesday 3 May

A great change ahead. Before the end of this month the whole of Changi camp has to be evacuated and we all move into the civil gaol (in and around it).

The gaol, built for 800, is to house 7,000 odd and the remainder of the P.O.W.s (including all those from upcountry at present in Singapore) will be in a hutted camp round the gaol. Officers and O.R.s are to be segregated and all is very much in the air at present as to what will happen to the Garden Control. We were told that all our complete garden area has to be abandoned – all except for the area which I have just taken over (about a fortnight ago) – quite a fertile patch, nearer to the gaol than the other garden areas and already planted (¾) with tapioca; the tamils were running it before me and they've been turned out.

'THE MOVE' overshadows everything, but, otherwise, items of news are: Mail in – in good quantity – just starting to be received in the camp – have got none so far: a step up in pay this month to $30.00 (not bad but with prices so big one is in much the same position as before).

Birthday on Friday. I'm going over to dine with Mike C. and taking over with me my tin of bully beef which I've been hanging on to for the last 18 months. Should go well wrapped up in tapioca pastry.

Less and less men on the gardens, as every available man is required for trailer parties.

Everything moveable in Changi has to go, including the wooden huts people live in. Gigantic problems of sanitation, water etc. have arisen and everyone in a bit of a flap. Except for three lorries permanently at the P.O.W.s disposal everything has to go up by trailer (distance to gaol about 1½ miles from main Changi camp gate).

It will be good to see the other fellows from upcountry – Alec and I are quite relishing the idea of rejoining the Gurkha Mess, if the G.C.G. packs up.

6 June

D-Day landings in Normandy

How do you mentally get through it?

We were fortunate in having information coming in. People were very courageous in keeping a home-made radio set – kept in the false bottom of a water bottle.

Our morale was always high and we were always going to get out by Christmas. "We can't possibly do another Christmas" was the cry. On the other hand the news came in, and it was all pathetically slow going: Mountbatten's lot creeping up and the Americans overrunning islands in the Pacific.

The chaps who organised these radio sets were very courageous because in doing so they were risking their lives. Very definitely. And the Japs knew we were getting information, and they said the risk would be death.

Getting the news in the evenings was quite a business. We used to assemble after dark, having posted sentries in one of the huts, and we would vary, of course, the hut we were going to hear the news – and we would creep in quite slowly, having posted our sentries to see there were no Japanese guards walking around. We would go in and the chap giving the news would start without any ado, and you would have to keep your ears pricked because he had to keep his voice low because the whole thing was not without risk. And he gave out the news. He was not the chap that owned the radio – he was probably two stages away from the radio chap. I am thinking of an Australian who had a tremendous memory and he spouted all this out – "I'll say this only once" – and then we all dispersed. And so we had a very good idea of what was going on.

No, morale wasn't always high. There were long spells when we wondered how long we were going to be there.

We put our trust in God that eventually we would come out OK.

Saturday 10 June

Having just caught a heavy cold, have not the energy or enthusiasm to write in much detail – but just a few notes on the past month's doings since it has seen the biggest changes since we have been P.O.W.s.

14th May: We (Garden Control) 'moved to gaol', self with severe tummy aches and feeling like death. Monday 15th: M.O. diagnosed me bacillary dysentery and sent me back to Hospital (Selarang Square). Van and Bob Durley followed me a day later – also dysentery – also Mavor. Felt quite fit after 2 days – discharged hospital. Tuesday 23rd: same day Bob Simpson came in as I left (dysentery).

My week in hospital quite a pleasant rest . After my return we remained in gaol another 4 or 5 days, then moved out into our present hut. 40 of us in attap hut: 2 beds touching, side by side, a gap of 3 feet, just giving room for small table, then another 2 beds together etc., etc. Down middle of hut a 2½ ft. corridor between ends of beds. Still – one gets used to anything! Got 8 letters last batch – just heard another 20 bags arrived. All Officers are living outside the gaol, in similar huts to ours and also in the coolie lines (senior officers).

Gardens: we have lost nearly 70 acres old gardens – new gardens stretch round near to sea with messing H.Q. right on coast at an unoccupied house – very pleasant position.

We all spent our half day afternoon down there last Wednesday in preference to sitting in our hut just outside the gaol wall; tide was up for bathing. Am taking my day off down there today.

We received a wireless message yesterday from Regimental Centre, dated Dec.'43 and were allowed to hand in a reply containing all our names – sincerely hope it fetches up.

15 & 16 June

US started bombing the iron and steel works in Yawata, Japan

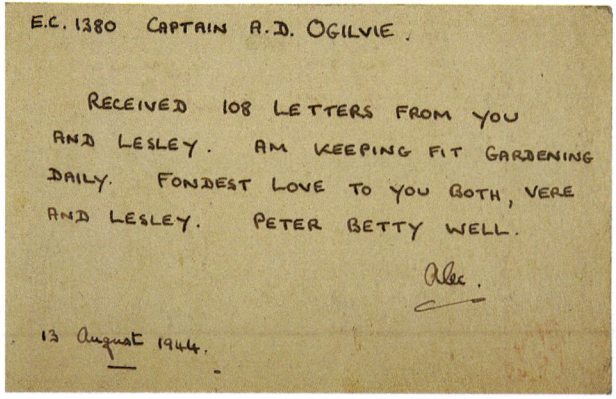

E.C. 1380   CAPTAIN A.D. OGILVIE .

RECEIVED 108 LETTERS FROM YOU AND LESLEY . AM KEEPING FIT GARDENING DAILY. FONDEST LOVE TO YOU BOTH, VERE AND LESLEY . PETER BETTY WELL .

Alec .

13 August 1944 .

Wednesday 18 October

Very nearly lost all interest in this and smoked the lot but suppose it may just possibly be of interest to someone. It's just been Gardens ... gardens since June last.

Quite a bit more mail but all finished now. Wrote our fourth postcard on 13th August – very glad to hear first two reached home.

The usual odd shows and gramophone concerts (but just now all are temporarily cancelled by order of I.J.A.).

Very little in rations – bulk of diet is greens off gardens. Total production last month 40 tons (a new high) of which my 4 acres produced about 5 tons. Just a few whitebait and lately the introduction of some soya beans. Canteen prices very high – Gula Malacca $5 per lb. – cheroots 16c each – java tobacco (if and when in) $1.70 per oz. One's pay barely permits keeping one in smokes only.

A general reshuffle of quarters a fortnight ago – Alec and I moved into a coolie quarter (great luxury!) with Fred Cross and Mike Cooper who is on the Air Strip organisation. The renewed privacy a great boon – small verandah for reading and messing, with room behind just large enough for 4 beds. Rather hot at night but getting used to it.

Before move used to take every Friday off down by the sea on Bob Darby's garden but now find it preferable to stay at home with a book.

Just had 2 days A.R.P. scheme – sirens blowing etc., interrupting work in gardens and black out at nights. Celebrating 2 years of the gardens tomorrow – all men having double vegetable rations for lunch.

Coconuts 85 cents each now (!) in canteen (not allowed to bring them in from outside the camp) – when they are available we generally split one four ways with our breakfast porridge – makes it very edible.

Poker in evenings still popular – never up or down very much.

Talks of possibility of a Red X ship arriving before Christmas – would make a wonderful difference, at this stage. Anyhow, Mike still has his one reserve tin of bully beef! – ate mine for last birthday.

Friday 27 October

Extremely heavy rains recently – not much damage on my plot. I.J.A. suddenly called for a performance of 'Autumn Crocus' last Monday evening (for which Alec and co. have been preparing for months now) – a dozen or so Japanese civilians present including some Tokyo theatre magnate. Personally enjoyed the play immensely – first straight play we have seen for many a month – the atmosphere of the Tyrol captured perfectly – the Innkeeper's part played by a Dutchman with very attractive accent.

All entertainments now greatly restricted by I.J.A. but they are allowing two performances a week of 'Autumn Crocus' at the Playhouse (the huge lavish theatre built inside the gaol – completed 6 weeks ago).

Excellent news – just heard 70 more bags of mail arrived – but believed to be mainly last year's. Had Derek R. up to eat with us the other night on our verandah, followed by bridge (excepting self – have not yet been caught) – rained very hard so no church. The privacy here compared to our old hut makes enormous difference to life.

```
                    "A U T U M N    C R O C U S".
                      A Play in Three Acts
                              by
                         Dodie Smith.

     Characters.                          Scene.
   In Order of appearance.
                                    An Inn in the Austrian Tyrol
  Andreas Steiner..........Hans Visser.        near Innsbruck.

  Liese..........Herman Van Del Linden.         ACT I.

  Miss Mayne................John Wood.    The Inn - Saturday Morning.

  Minna....................Harry Wise.          ACT II.

  Edith...................Niel Maccoll.   Scene 1. The Inn - Saturday Evening.

  Fanny...................Ronnie Lewis.   Scene 2. The Shrine on the Mountain -
                                                  Early Sunday Morning.
  Alaric..................Alec Ogilvie.

  Audrey.................Keith Stevens.          ACT III.

  Rev.Edward Mayne........R.H.Pantling.   The Inn - Sunday Morning.

  Herr Feldmann...........Kenneth Luke.     0-0-0-0-0-0-0-0-0-0-0

  Frau Feldmann...........Roel Meyer.     Produced by Osmond Daltry.

                  0-0-0-0-0-0-0-0-0-0-0-0-0-0-0

                  Produced at the Playhouse Theatre,
                       Changi, October, 1944.
                  0-0-0-0-0-0-0-0-0-0-0-0-0-0-0
```

The Playhouse Theatre

PRESENTS

Autumn Crocus

By

dodie smith

PRODUCED BY OSMOND DALTRY

CHANGI P.O.W CAMP

OCTOBER 1944

Monday 6 November

AT LAST – at long last: yesterday – Sunday – the best Guy Fawkes Day I've ever known. We were down in the gardens at about 10.15 when the 'Brown out' siren sounded – didn't take much notice – thought it was a practice; five minutes later the 'Black out' went and our Korean sentry ordered us all to collect together under some coconuts – also according to previous practices. Shortly after heard bursts of Ack-ack and a few large planes were visible – very high – obviously not Japanese – about 25 or 30 in all and a lot of Ack-ack.

The first allied planes we have seen since Feb.'42.

Two of them wheeled right overhead and their 4 engines visible – all very enthralling. Yanks here cannot decide whether they were Liberators or B. 29s. Hope to God they follow it up before long.

A little mail trickling in from the 70 bags but mostly 1943 stuff. Missed my day off last week so taking today instead. Run out of money already this month owing to overspending last month – no cheroots till December!

Sunday 12 November

Couple of large allied planes over again last Wednesday – very high – but no fireworks. Observed 2 minutes silence out on garden yesterday at 11 a.m. (with the Japanese 'Temple' call instead of the last-post) – was also our 1,000th day as P.O.W.s! A combined Armistice Day Commemoration Service this evening in the gaol theatre.

17 November

US B29 Super-fortress bombers, deployed from Mariana Islands in the Pacific, started strategic bombing of Japan.

Wednesday 22 November

Things getting a bit tight all round. Our weekly issue of one free ounce of tobacco (local stuff) has stopped. Cheroots have risen to 25 cents each and only very limited quantity of them. So I have had to cut out smoking altogether – for the time being anyhow – have had no smoke for last five days – am almost used to it during day but it comes very trying at nights.

Coconuts very scarce and now $1.00 each.

Another large allied plane came over two days ago in the evening just as we were about to have our evening meal – quite low – brown out did not sound till it had almost passed out of sight.

Quite a considerable competition these days with the little garden patches in our 'suburbia'. Our patch is about 10ft. × 10ft. with some good looking tomatoes coming on – 2 chilli plants, 2 brinjals and some Ceylon spinach – will all help to swell our meagre diet (if we are here long enough?!)

Seem to be steadily losing weight these days – not surprising I suppose if one is never satisfied by any meal; still consider myself lucky to be on gardens, with a good vegetable ration for lunch.

Thursday 21 December

Christmas Day next Monday – seems we may not do so badly after all in the food line. We four also making our own private cake for which all arrangements now fully in hand.

Another consignment of toys sent this year to the children in Sime Road.

Garden still going strong: extending mine with an 'orchard' of bananas and papayas – the former rather depressing to have to plant at this stage.

My weight now only just over 9 stone – hope it won't fall much lower.

Canteen prices still rising (coconuts now $1.40 each; peanuts $13 per 1b !!)

We have been supplementing our Wednesday and Sunday lunches with tapioca (at $1.10 per lb.) and coconut, where possible. Still get a bulky lunch down on gardens.

Now ration myself to one smoke only for day – a cheroot in the evening – and the stub carves up to make a cigarette. Lately had attacks of going septic at slightest scratch – extremely annoying. Mail – a much later batch in; have received cards up to July this year saying my third card got home, in which I said home letters were fetching up – very satisfactory. Cannot understand Mervyn's movements.

Spell of very cold weather last few days; rain today – no garden; sort of day at home for toffee making in the morning and walk followed by enormous tea in afternoon, by the fire.

1945

Sunday 28 January

Paper very scarce now – so making this effusion very sketchy. Xmas and the New Year passed off extremely well, with wonderfully high spirits shown throughout the camp even more than the preceding two years. Our men overfed us magnificently and our own cake was a brilliant success.

The Xmas Pantomine in gaol theatre provided good amusement. (They are now doing three of the 'Tonight at 8.30' plays (N. Coward) – some of the best acting that has been produced in Changi).

B. 29s have been over again this month – once in numbers and 2 or 3 occasions when a single plane or two have come over; the first occasion was the full show of bombs and ack-ack etc. – all highly entertaining – we get as thrilled as small children whenever the sirens go.

The most recent valuable addition to life has been the sale at the canteen of palm oil, at a reasonable price – makes a vast difference to the breakfast 'pap' – we also are able to have the occasional 'fry-up' for lunch and in the evening – quite apart, of course, from its great vitamin value.

Camp at present completely out of smokes – very trying but expected to be remedied shortly.

We are incidentally also out of 'bumph'! Up till now there has been a constant supply of old American newspapers but even they have failed – all pointing to the conclusion that it's high time we got out of this place.

Alec got his name over in the Xmas broadcast (sang a song) – and we were all given a 25 word cable early this month – sincerely hope they reached home – feel very doubtful about it.

Still the same old gardening – day in, day out.

Mail has cut out completely – shouldn't be surprised if we didn't get any more, now.

Our little patch of tomatoes were amazingly successful – must have had over 400 off the odd dozen plants.

Saturday 13 March

Very little worth committing to paper. Life getting very grim these days – just had a heavy cut in rations, ie. down to 9½ oz. rice per head per day. Am fortunately on the heavy duty scale (having an outside job) but even so, the difference is very noticeable. One feels very 'whacked' after a full day out.

Getting increasingly difficult to supplement meals as tapioca is now up to $2.30 per lb., and palm oil very scarce. BUT a Red X boat came in about a week ago (long awaited) and we hope to get the food in a fortnight or so – should help things considerably.

Daily meals at present: breakfast – 1 pint 'pap' (rice porridge), lunch – ½ to ¾ pint hash, evening – 1 pint hash (better than lunch) and one 'doover' (rissole). Light duty lunch (if one happens to be in camp) contains no rice at all – just ¼ pint vegetable stew.

Fortunately one can still afford to smoke which does a bit to keep hunger at bay.

Air Raids Saturday, 24th February, Friday, 2nd March and two more since then but no sign of an allied plane for past week. I.J.A. have closed down the main camp theatre but still have occasional small shows in Officers' lines.

No news of mail on the Red X ship – doubt whether we shall ever get any more now. Becoming infinitely weary of it all but lucky to maintain fitness – my weight last week 9 stone 4 lbs. – fully expect to go under 9 stone very shortly! (Alcc dramatically announces he is now under 11 stone in first time since aged 9 or thereabouts!) Going hard to produce vegetables on our little home patch – tomatoes no good for bulk – putting in Ceylon spinach and bayam; made our little extension in space last Sunday – hard at it from 2 till 5 p.m. and completely exhausted ourselves – but well worth the trouble. We are trying out all kinds of things for food these days, including seaweed, snails (fried), chick-weed (growing wild as our chief weed on the gardens) and leaves off the hibiscus hedges. There appears to be no limit to what is edible!

Had a very vivid skiing dream last night – next Xmas, maybe?!

Clothing getting difficult now – especially towels (serviceable ones practically nonexistent). Hear there is some wonderful American clothing on this ship but not enough to go round. But there appears to be no limit to the possibilities of repairing and patching.

Shirt situation not too bad as one wears nothing up top all day long until after the evening shower. Some of us on the gardens have a very fortunate source of salt – the sea (instead of 3.50 a lb. at the canteen). Sugar incidentally, is now quite impossible $17.60 a 1b. – almost one's months pay! – and coconuts are up to $2.40 each. Sweet potatoes $3.60 per 1b. So $20 a month pay (after paying messing sub.) doesn't go very far. 20 cents for a small cheroot which 18 months ago was 1 cent.

To bed – all putting our faith in the Red X food fetching up.

Saturday 31 March

Was called upon, at very short notice, to go with a working party (about 600 strong) ordered by the Japs to proceed to another camp – not known which. After 1½ hours lorry drive, found ourselves at Kranji (north of the island, near Causeway), wired off from the rest of the camp as we were nothing to do with the Hospital. The other ranks went out daily – work mainly tunnelling into the ground – much speculation as to what the tunnels were to be used for. Officers not allowed outside the camp. Treatment whilst at work generally good, though occasional instances of usual bashings etc. A great increase in rations compared to Changi, and the men received extra tapioca and smokes out on the job.

I got a small garden going, providing sufficient green vegetables to be of value to our little sub-camp hospital. Quantity of rations gradually decreased and condition of men's clothing and footwear became very bad indeed. A small consignment of Red X boxes (which were pooled) helped things out. News of the Atomic Bomb and Russia, and anything seemed possible.

8 May: Germany surrenders

6 August: USA drops atomic bomb on Hiroshima

9 August: USA drops atomic bomb on Nagasaki

The End

Whilst hacking at my garden, 11th August, heard the news that the Japanese were prepared to accept the terms of Potsdam Declaration. Following day heard that there were two provisos and it seemed quite possible that the whole thing might fall through – nerves on edge for three days, until the Jap commandant came in and told us officially that the 'war had finished'.

Followed a fortnight or more of waiting (until the incoming troops arrived), during which time the Japs unearthed large quantities of Red X food and clothing which they must have been sitting on for many months.

15 August: Japan surrender in Singapore

2 September: Japan sign the Surrender document

Thursday 6 September

Joined up with our Gurkhas in their camp in south of the island.

Sunday 9 September

Main part of battalion sailed for India.

Thursday 13 September

Got on a boat and sailed to Calcutta with remaining 80 men of the battalion.

P.K.B.

LETTERS HOME

Sunday 9 September 1945

from Singapore

My dearest Mum and Dad,

I've been awaiting this opportunity for such a long time – of being able to write you a proper letter – that now the occasion has at long last come, I scarcely know how to begin – it's all so overwhelming.

The first thing to report, anyway, is that I am <u>extremely</u> fit, and I only hope to God that you are both likewise. Been putting on weight rapidly during the last fortnight, since we started getting Red X food (a great change from the eternal rice!) and now clock over 10 stone. We wrote 5 postcards in all – so hope that you got them. Your continued efforts of letters & cards were magnificent they honestly were – and I was always envied as being a receiver of more than my share!

Have not seen Alec Ogilvie for past 5 months as I was moved to another smaller camp, but I know he is fit and O.K. – I fully realise that you both must have suffered great anxieties on my behalf, but Mervyn used to tell me frequently in his cards how magnificently you bore it all – a thousand congratulations & thanks.

I have never had any real hardships the whole 3 and half years as I never once left Singapore Island – where you probably guessed I was. The old job of gardening was a damned good choice – gave me a permanent and interesting daily occupation and made the time pass doubly quickly – also kept fit with the exercise and daily extra greens, etc – 'garden stew'!

But now it's all over – mighty hard to realise!

Managed to get down yesterday to see our men in their camp – all seem to be in v. good heart and overjoyed at seeing us again – no knowing yet as to whether we will sail back with them or not – anyhow presume I will go Dehra Dun at first and then HOME with not too much delay – must see Mervyn – hope I'm able to contact him and that he is not in some ungetatable war zone. So much I still want to say but we still have restrictions. Just burning to see you both and all Barbara's large family.

All my profoundest love – Peter

Singapore.   7th Sept 45

My dearest Mum & Dad,

I've been awaiting this opportunity for such a long time – of being able to write you a proper letter – that now the occasion has at long last come, I scarcely know how to begin – its all so overwhelming. The first thing to report, anyway, is that I am extremely fit, and I only hope to God that you are both likewise? Been putting on weight rapidly during the last fortnight, since we started getting Red X food (a great change from the eternal rice!) and now clock over 10 stone. We wrote 5 postcards in all – so hope that you got them. Your combined efforts of letters & cards were magnificent they honestly were – and I was always envied as being a receiver of more than my share! Have not seen Alec Baillie for some 5 months as I was moved to another smaller camp, but I know he is fit & O.K. – I fully realize that you both must have suffered great anxieties on my behalf, but Merryn used to tell me frequently, in his cards how magnificently you bore it all – a thousand congratulations & thanks. I have never had any real torture, hardships the whole 3½ years, as I never once left Singapore behind – where you probably guessed I was. The old job of gardening was a damned good choice – gave me a permanent & interesting daily occupation, & made the time pass doubly quickly – also kept fit with the exercise and daily extra greens, etc – garden stew! But now its all over – mighty hard to realize! Time has dragged a bit heavy since we initially heard of the end, but now hoping to get on board a boat almost any day. Managed to send a letter off to Merryn today via some Americans who were reputed to be leaving by air for Calcutta – also our standard telegrams went today – sincerely hope you will have got it by now. By the way I got your photo, Mum – excellent I thought – only wish

Wednesday 19 September 1945

on board ship to Calcutta

Just prior to our departure, Admiral the Lord Mountbatten (and his wife) paid a visit to our camp – spoke in Urdu to the men and then a 5 minute talk to the Officers on his victorious Burma show – we were all impressed by him (on his personality).

Well, the 'great day' of which we have thought about so much, for so long, is shortly to become a reality – still find it difficult to realise it is all over. Hope Nelly still going strong – give her my love – she'd better mix that Christmas pudding as I thoroughly intend – come what may – to be at home for Christmas.

Wonder what chances of Switzerland this winter?! Cannot see why it shouldn't be possible – so hoping M. will be able to get some home leave.

COURAGE, FRIENDSHIP AND LOYALTY

Together they had endured extreme stress, fatigue and loss fighting the Japanese down the length of Malaya. They supported each other through the horrid times and those early days in captivity when many were badly treated. Upon their release, every man sang the praises of his comrades. It was more than just courage that carried them through those dark days; friendship and loyalty played a crucial role, just as it did among the Gurkha soldiers.

A good example of this support for one another can be seen in the letter written by Major Evans, Second-in-Command of the regiment. 'Uncle', as he was affectionately known amongst the officers, took time to write to Peter's mother in Camberley:

> I would like you to know how well he did, both in the campaign and in POW life. He was to Geoffrey Woollcombe and myself and later also to Derek Robertson a tower of strength and one who was so reliable and cool under the most adverse conditions.

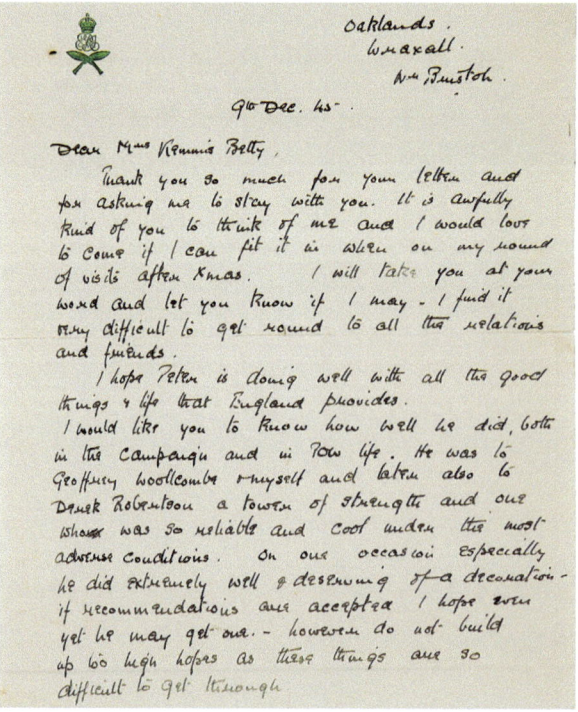

LIFE AFTER CHANGI

Alec and Peter had done far more than simply survive the rigours of being prisoners of war. Thanks to their exceptional organisational skills and persuasive leadership in managing the Changi vegetable gardens, countless prisoners were spared from death. From the very beginning of their captivity, securing enough food was the primary focus. Prisoners were dying, not only from malnutrition but also from diseases brought on by a lack of proper nourishment.

They were grateful to have played a meaningful role in helping to feed the thousands of prisoners who passed through Changi. The efforts of those who managed and worked in the gardens were never properly recognised, either at the time or since. Perhaps Peter's Singapore diary will, in some way, help bring attention to the vital work of those who helped save so many lives.

Alec Ogilvie returned home to England as part of the main party with most of the battalion.

Peter stayed behind in Malaya to collect other survivors of the battalion who had been imprisoned outside Singapore. He returned to India with 80 of the remaining Gurkhas, travelling via Calcutta before arriving once more in the foothills of the Himalayas at Dehra Dun. He was granted six months' leave. Unlike Alec, he hadn't had a girlfriend before the war, so he went to stay with sister Barbara in southern India before finally returning home.

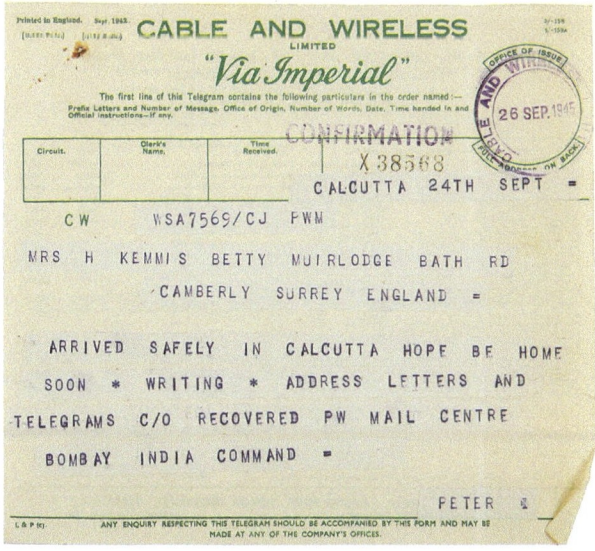

Before Alec left London for India in 1938, he promised his girlfriend, Lesley Woollan, that he would marry her and assured his parents he would return from Calcutta to do so. However, World War Two, the fight against the Japanese and his subsequent imprisonment delayed his plans. As soon as the war ended, he set the date for 17th November 1945. At the time, he was still an officer in the 2nd King Edward's Own Gurkha Rifles and duly married in uniform. Peter, who was on leave at the time, was asked to be his best man.

Alec's wedding to Lesley, with Peter as best man

Peter made the most of his time back in England, reconnecting with friends and, in 1946, meeting and falling in love with Gemma St. Maur. However, at the end of his leave, he was sent straight back to India, posted as Second-in-Command to the 5th Battalion in Razmak, Waziristan, where he remained until the battalion was disbanded in January 1947.

On 22nd February, whilst on leave in the UK, Peter married Miss Gemma St Maur. Perhaps not entirely unrelated to Peter's love of skiing, they honeymooned in Switzerland. He then rejoined the 2nd Battalion, King Edward's Own Gurkha Rifles at Dinapore in northern India.

In March 1948, Peter Kemmis Betty accompanied the 2nd Battalion to Malaya and served with 2GR during the Emergency, a campaign aimed at limiting communist insurgency. His familiarity with the area was invaluable, as the 2nd Gurkhas were once again based in Ipoh. By late December 1952, Peter had become CO of A Company, stationed at Chemor, just north of Ipoh. One of his notable achievements was organising a large-scale tree-planting exercise, principally with Gold Mohur trees, at the Sirmoor Barracks. Known as 'flame trees', the bright red flowers added a much-needed splash of colour to the barracks.

For his efforts in combatting the communist insurgents, Peter was one of three members of the battalion awarded the Perak Meritorious Service Medal (Pingat Jasa Malaysia) in 1954.

During their time in Ipoh, Peter and Gemma made many wonderful friends and enjoyed everything that Malaya had to offer. Off-duty, they spent weekends in the Cameron Highlands or at Port Dickson on the coast. They also started a family, with Richard born in Batu Gajah in 1952 and Charles in Ipoh in 1954.

After a year as GSO3 to the Gurkha Infantry Brigade, the whole family set sail aboard HMT Empire Windrush to return home from Singapore. Unfortunately, all was not right with the ship, and passing through the Suez Canal the captain reported a problem in the engine room. Disaster struck in the Mediterranean when, on 30th March 1954, the ship caught fire at 6.30 a.m. The family had an inside cabin and didn't hear the explosion, but Peter was up early and, sensing something was not right, went up on deck to explore. He immediately saw that the rear funnel was belching smoke and was instructed to get the family and move to the lifeboat stations. Mercifully, Peter, Gemma and their two sons (aged just 2 years and 6 months, respectively) were rescued before the boat sank off the coast of Algeria. All their luggage and possessions were lost at sea. Everything they had was gone.

The next chapter of his life began when he rejoined the 2nd Battalion in Hong Kong as 2IC. In February 1956, he commanded the advance party, which moved to Singapore and then onwards to Kuala Pilah in Negri Sembilan to resume operations against the Communist terrorists. After UK leave, in May 1958 Peter was very proud to be appointed as Commandant of the 2nd King Edward's Own Gurkha Rifles. He was mentioned in despatches in April 1959 for his services while the battalion was operating in Johore during the final months of the Malayan Emergency. It was his greatest honour to command the Gurkhas whom he held in such high regard.

Silver kukri in sheaf
Presented to Lt. Col. P. Kemmis Betty MC
by all ranks, 2nd BN 2nd K.E.O. Goorkhas,
on his relinquishing command 1960

Peter Kemmis Betty

Peter returned to a peaceful family life back in England in 1960, though there was a great deal of excitement when he was offered and then accepted the position of Military Attache in Kathmandu, Nepal.

This was to be a most wonderful three years back in the Himalayas. Peter felt at home in the mountains, and being back in Nepal meant he could stay in touch with many of the Gurkha soldiers who had endured such tough times fighting the Japanese. One of the main responsibilities of the Military Attache in Kathmandu was to be the eyes and ears of the Embassy, and this meant he could get out walking in the hills and talking to his Gurkha friends in the villages north and west of Pokhara. The family often accompanied him trekking in the foothills of Annapurna where he would enter villages to a welcoming party and an insistence that the whole family would join the elders for an evening meal that often included excellent hospitality with much Raksi consumed. Many stories were told.

Wanting to give something back to the courageous hill people he had served with, Peter volunteered to join a party of climbers Sir Edmund Hillary organised to help build a school at Lukla, in the Everest Region. It was typical of Peter that he was prepared to roll up his sleeves and get down to some hard work, albeit amongst the mountains he so loved and for the benefit of the hill people that he found to be so incredibly loyal.

Gemma and Peter could not have enjoyed their three years in Nepal more and they returned back to England in time for their third son, David, to be born in August 1967.

*

Meanwhile, Alec was about to begin a new chapter in his life. Shortly after getting married, his discharge papers came through and he was released from the Army. He and Lesley returned to Calcutta, where he resumed his career with Andrew Yule.

The late 1940s were a time of great upheaval in India. Hindu-Muslim riots and massacres in Calcutta in 1946 foreshadowed the widespread violence and mass migrations that followed the Partition of India and Pakistan in August 1947. By 1948, Alec had returned in time to assist Andrew Yule in its transition to becoming a public company.

Alec remained in Calcutta, but given the unsettled times Lesley returned to the UK at the end of 1947 so that their first son, Adam, could be born in England rather than India. He arrived in March 1948.

Despite India's Independence, expatriate family life in Calcutta during the 1950s saw little change. In these relatively quieter times, their second son, Graham, was born in September 1951. Life continued to revolve around social and sporting clubs, while homes were well staffed with lifelong loyal servants. The departure of a family from India was often a deeply emotional event for all involved.

One of the most devoted amongst them was Man Bahadur Thapa (also known as Bobby), a Nepali who had started working for Alec before the war. Alec reconnected with him in 1946, and when the Ogilvie family left Calcutta in 1965 he ensured that Bobby and his family received a pension for life.

Alec was a highly successful businessman and by the time he became Managing Director in 1956, Andrew Yule had grown into a vast conglomerate with interests spanning across north-east India. What began with tea plantations in Darjeeling and Assam, followed by cotton spinning in Bengal, had expanded into engineering, power generation and chemicals. Alec served as Chairman from 1962 to 1965. During his tenure as Chairman, Alec became one of the last British businessmen in India to be elected President of the Associated Chambers of Commerce of India. He also served as President of the Bengal Chamber of Commerce, taking on significant national responsibilities and forging high profile connections. His leadership culminated in hosting Prime Minister, Lal Bahadur Shastri, at an event, during which he proudly wore his Gurkha tie. In recognition of his contributions to industry and commerce, Alec was knighted by the Queen in July 1965.

After returning to England, Alec remained deeply engaged in business becoming Chairman of Powell Duffryn in 1969, a role he assumed while once again wearing his Gurkha tie on the day he became Chairman.

Even after retiring in 1978, he stayed active as a member of the Council of King Edward VII's Hospital for Officers. His brief service in the 2nd Gurkhas left a lasting impression and on nearly all formal occasions he continued to wear his Gurkha tie as a mark of pride and remembrance.

In the later years, Peter and Alec saw little of each other, despite Alec and his family living in Sussex and Peter in Hampshire. Many veterans and their loved ones, having heard the horrific stories of mistreatment of British prisoners-of-war by the Japanese, were reluctant to speak about those dark days. Alec's wife, aware of the emotional toll that three and a half years as a British POW had taken on her husband, preferred not to discuss Changi. For a time, she also refused to have any Japanese products in the house.

Alec Ogilvie second from right

Though Alec's time in the Gurkhas was relatively short, he developed a lasting admiration for the soldiers he fought alongside in Malaya and Singapore. He remained a devoted member of the 2nd Gurkhas' regimental association, the Sirmoor Club, from its creation until his death in 1984. Peter and Alec continued to meet at these Sirmoor Club gatherings once or twice a year, but visits to their home in Sussex were sadly discouraged.

When news of Alec's passing reached him, Peter was deeply saddened. He wrote most of the eulogy and attended the funeral. Despite having seen little of each other in their later years, it was a painful occasion, given the close bond they had shared.

Alec Ogilvie remained his best friend.

*

And you might well ask, "Why 'Half a Banana'?" Over the years, whenever asked if he might like something, Peter would typically ask for half, be it fruit, a cake or a roll. This was not due to lack of appetite, but because Changi had instilled in him the habit of sharing his food or saving some in the hope that there might be a little left for later.

In time, it became a fond family tradition, always met with a knowing smile. Ordinarily, Peter was most content with just 'Half a Banana'.